The Desires of
Your Heart

Financial Giving and the Spiritual Life

Results of a Congregational Study
By Christian Community, Inc.
Report by Holly Carcione, Steve Clapp,
Kristen Leverton, Angela Zimmerman

The Desires of Your Heart -
Financial Giving and the Spiritual Life

Results of a Congregational Study by Christian Community, Inc.
Report by Holly Carcione, Steve Clapp, Kristen Leverton, Angela Zimmerman

The Desires of Your Heart artwork on the cover is by Patricia Kennedy Helman and Rosanna McFadden.

Biblical quotations, unless otherwise noted, are from the New Revised Standard Version, © 1989 by the Division of Christian Education of the National Council of Churches of Christ in the United States of America, and are used by permission.

The authors of this book and the publisher are not accountants or attorneys. The information on church and individual finances provided in this report is accurate to the best of our knowledge at the time of printing, but these are complex matters subject to changing tax codes and other government regulations. You always want to check with a certified public accountant or an attorney before making fundamental changes in your church or personal financial systems.

"Trust in the LORD, and do good;
so you will live in the land
and enjoy security.
Take delight in the LORD,
and he will give you
the desires of your heart."

Psalm 37:3-4 [NRSV]

"You shall love the LORD your God
with all your heart,
and with all your soul,
and with all your strength,
and with all your mind;
and your neighbor as yourself."

Luke 10:27 [NRSV]

Contents

*This book is respectfully dedicated
to the many people who cooperated with us
in the Spirituality and Giving Project
and
to the millions of people
who support their congregations and other causes
in joyful response to God's grace –
and in so doing move closer
to the best and truest desires of their hearts.*

What's Happening To the Money?

"The church has to let one of the associate pastors go in January," said Jim to two clergy friends of other denominations at breakfast. They were meeting to plan a cooperative Thanksgiving service, but the conversation had turned to church finances. "Our membership has been in decline for several years, but our giving stayed good – really better than the rate of inflation – until last year. Last year we not only didn't keep pace with inflation, we actually had a loss in giving, down about seven percent from the year before. This year we've been running seven to eight percent down. That's about a fifteen percent drop in two years, and there's no reason to think next year will be better."

"Are people unhappy about something?" asked Frank.

"No, they aren't unhappy – or at least that doesn't seem to be the reason giving is down. When we've lost members in the past, our old faithful have simply dug a little deeper to keep the church fiscally sound. But we've lost so many of our life-long members through death and through moves to retirement locations that the faithful who are left can't pick up what's been lost. This year one of our most loyal members died in February. He was giving a hundred dollars a week. Our treasurer tells me that the total amount of the pledges from four new families who came into our church doesn't equal a hundred dollars a week. The

people who've been joining us don't seem as committed to the congregation as our older members, and the younger ones don't have as much money. We need to find some strategy to shake more money loose, or we're going to have continuing cuts in staff and program."

"Have you tried an every member visitation for pledges?" Teresa asked. Younger than Jim and Frank, she is in her third year pastoring a congregation much smaller than Jim's declining one or Frank's growing one.

"As a matter of fact," Jim responded, "we have. In the past the congregation has done a visitation every six or seven years. The process of training people and having them make personal visits to every family in the church to get pledges used to be very effective. We started another visitation last fall, but we ended up changing our strategy. We just couldn't get enough volunteers to make it work. We're low on money, and we're low on workers."

"We're not low on people," Frank offered. "We keep growing, but our giving leaves a lot to be desired. People want all kinds of programs and a high level of service, but they don't understand how expensive it is to offer so much and to maintain a large staff. Then we have people who belong to our church or at least attend our church every week – and who also are involved in another church. We have three families who come to us because of our children and youth programs and go to First Presbyterian for their music program. I don't know how First Presbyterian feels about it, but I wish the families weren't dividing their attendance and their giving. It doesn't feel fair to either congregation. They see the church through the eyes of a consumer rather than feeling a part of the body of Christ."

"Do you know what your individual members give to the church?" Jim asked. "I've been trying to get our treasurer to share that with me for two years, and I haven't gotten anywhere with it."

"Of course I know," said Frank. "How can you pastor and help people spiritually if you don't know how generous they are? I'm always careful not to put individuals on the spot about their giving, but knowing what people give makes possible a lot of subtle reinforcements for them and for the congregation itself."

"If you could only get people to talk about money," Teresa offered. "People in my church don't want to discuss money – no matter what the context."

"I know that's part of our problem too," agreed Jim. "We feel so uncomfortable talking about money that we avoid the topic except when we're setting the budget and doing the annual campaign. It's a crucial part of the spiritual life that we simply neglect most of the year."

"I read one article which stated that giving in our denomination and most others is still going up," Teresa shared, "and I read another that says people are actually giving less. That's confusing. What's really happening?"

What's Happening?

What's really happening with giving? Jim, Teresa, and Frank aren't alone in wondering about that. Giving patterns have been changing in churches all over the United States and Canada, and the strategies which have been effective with past generations are not always producing the same results today. Even the statistical information we receive is sometimes confusing.

For the most part, overall giving in most congregations in North America has continued to rise annually even though membership in many denominations has declined. Many generous people have made that possible. The 1997 edition of the *Yearbook of American and Canadian Churches* includes statistics comparing the 1994 year with the 1995 year for fifteen denominations; fourteen of the fifteen show increases in giving, in some instances by as much as fourteen percent. [The *Yearbook* gives statistical information for more than a hundred U.S. denominations and more than fifty Canadian denominations, but consistency in categories and reporting means that valid comparisons can't be made for all of those. The overall trend, however, is increased giving across most of the denominations reporting.]

As leaders in most congregations and denominations are aware, however, all is not well. There are four especially significant factors which contribute to our uneasiness:

1. Studies on the giving habits of

individual Christians show that church giving as a percentage of personal income has been declining for years. Many people have increased their giving, but they are increasing it at a lower rate than their rising income rates. That was probably the topic of the second article referred to by Teresa. This continued drop in percentage is a significant cause for concern. If personal incomes had not been rising, total church income would unquestionably have declined.

The best research in this area has been done by John and Sylvia Ronsvalle, who produce an annual statistical analysis called The State of Church Giving, *and who have written an insightful book titled* Behind the Stained Glass Windows: Money Dynamics in the Church *[Baker Books]. They direct The Empty Tomb, Inc. in Champaign, Illinois, and have had years of involvement in direct ministries with the poor.*

2. Under financial pressure and with the need to devote more resources to improved internal programming and their own outreach to nonmembers, many congregations are not giving as generously to missions and other causes beyond their own congregational needs. Most national and regional denominational agencies and missions are feeling the sting of reduced income. It's taking more money proportionately to maintain and hopefully expand the program of the local congregation.

3. The reason that membership decline in many congregations has not resulted in decreased giving is that other members pick up the difference. Those who pick up the difference are often older members of the congregation with well-developed giving habits, and those persons are aging. There are many congregations like the one pastored by Jim, which experienced a crucial year when the tide turned and there were no longer enough of those loyal, older members to keep finances from declining.

4. Some of the "tried and true" methods of fund-raising in congregations are not producing the same results today as they did one or two decades ago. Those who are boomers and younger simply do not respond to unified budgets and every member visitations in the same way that many older persons have over the years.

Consider, for example, what happened in the United Methodist Church between 1973 and 1994:

- Total purchasing power (adjusted for inflation) across the denomination as a whole **increased** by more than ten percent.

- Purchasing power of funds for health insurance, pensions, and other benefits **increased** about nine percent.

- Purchasing power of most categories of benevolent funds **decreased** by at last twenty-five percent.

(The above information is based on published statistics of the United Methodist Church.)

Similar patterns are evident across most mainline denominations. These realities are having significant impact on church bureaucracies, missions, and other agencies outside of the local church. Faced with increasing internal financial needs, local churches find it difficult to become motivated to give as generously to missions and other benevolent programs outside the local church as in the past. Congregations and their pastors are faced with extremely tough decisions about their budgets and their financial campaigns. Those responsible for fund-raising for denominational and ecumenical church agencies find themselves confronting many difficult challenges.

Consequences of Shrinking Benevolence Dollars

Let's go from the breakfast meeting of Jim, Teresa, and Frank to the luncheon meeting of Janet, Tom, and Barbara, who are talking about cosponsoring a stewardship workshop for congregations in their region.

Janet is the director of a church agency which works with troubled children and their families. In the nineteen-forties, fifties, and sixties, the agency focused on adoptions. The seventies brought a gradual transition to the work with abused and neglected children, which continues to be its focus. "Until we got into the nineties, seventy percent of our money came directly from the denomination. Now the figure is forty percent, and it's likely to keep falling. It's becoming harder and harder for us to pick up the sixty percent plus that the denomination doesn't provide."

"I can identify with that," said Tom, who directs an ecumenical campus ministry. "That's why this workshop is important to all of us. My campus ministry used to raise about twenty percent of its budget and get the other eighty percent from four supporting denominations. Today we get about thirty percent from the denominations and have to raise the other seventy percent locally. That's increasingly difficult to do."

"And these days I don't even feel secure about my own salary and benefits," offered Barbara, who is in a regional staff position in the denomination. "We also don't have the money we need to do our work. I've got two pastors in trouble right now who desperately need some time out of the parish and some money for counseling. A decade ago we could have handled that through denominational funds. Now the money isn't there. Do we force them to resign and go into another line of work so they can afford counseling?"

"It isn't realistic to think that we can keep raising ever-increasing sums of money directly from churches and individuals," said Janet. "At some point we need the denomination to start doing more again."

"But that isn't going to happen," responded Barbara. "You have trouble raising it from congregations, but it isn't any easier for the denomination to do it. You have the advantage of being able to do slick brochures with pictures of the cute children who benefit from your programs and ministries. My picture in a brochure with the title 'Barbara Taylor, Church Bureaucrat' isn't going to motivate anyone to give more money to the denomination."

All three laughed. Then Tom observed,

"When I think about my own home congregation, I realize that denominational loyalty doesn't count for much anymore – especially not in terms of finances. People have to be sold on the importance of what you're doing. They have to feel like their money, given to or through you, is making a difference. They are not going to give just because one of our organizations wants them to."

"And there's a tendency to take the denominational structure for granted," said Barbara. "People just assume that positions like mine are always going to be there, even though that isn't necessarily the case. It isn't very exciting to support a church bureaucracy, but someone has to do it, especially when it comes to coordinating the search process between pastors and churches. I'd like to see changes in the bureaucracy myself, but I don't see how we can do without jobs like mine."

Janet asked, "What about giving motivated by faith in Christ and commitment to the church? What about teaching people to trust the process in the denomination to make decisions about how money is utilized? Can't people be helped to see the virtues in that kind of giving and that kind of trust?"

"If we're going to do that in most congregations," Tom said, "then we're going to have to make a lot of changes – and we're going to have to talk more openly about money, which we don't want to do."

"What I want to know," Janet pondered, "is how much we should be focusing on gifts for our endowment and memorials. Our church-related colleges are putting us all to shame. They just keep on raising more and more money, especially through endowments. Agencies like mine don't do nearly as well."

"And local churches don't either," observed Tom. "I know four relatively wealthy people in my home congregation who are leaving substantial money to our church-related college but aren't doing anything comparable for the congregation, for causes like my campus ministry, or for overseas missions. The colleges have full-time development staff and can nurture that giving in a way a campus ministry or children's agency does not. Our church-related college pays their top development officer more than the entire budget for my ecumenical campus ministry. Pastors and congregational volunteers find it more difficult to talk as directly about wills, memorials, and endowments than trained development officers find it."

"It feels to me like we face a transition," Janet said. "As some of our very dedicated older church members die, we're going to have a gap before younger members develop the kinds of giving habits that their parents and grandparents have. If we were getting more from endowments, wills, livings trusts, and memorials, that could help our churches and agencies like mine make it through that transition."

Transition

Transition. That word conveys a great deal of what is happening in the life of congregations and denominations today. While the focus of this report is on stewardship, there are many other transitions in process in most congregations and denominations; and many of those other transitions have impact on the financial situation of local churches. For example:

- The transition to large numbers of congregations which are not affiliated with any particular denomination. Coast to coast, the last twenty years have brought a dramatic increase in the number of independent churches which have grown to impressive size.

- The transition, in general, to more and more people choosing larger congregations which can offer a wider range of programming than a small or medium-sized church.

- The transition in denominational loyalty with people choosing a local church not because of its denominational affiliation but because of the programs and services it offers. The fact that someone is raised Presbyterian, Baptist, Lutheran, or Episcopalian does not guarantee that person will stay in that tradition. Even very stable, heavily family-based churches like the Mennonite and Brethren traditions are finding that denominational loyalty is no longer automatic or reliable.

- The transition of the meaning of church membership from participation in the body of Christ to consumerism. Increasing numbers of people see the selection of a church having much in common with the selection of a regular restaurant, a country club, a shopping center, or a car dealership. The analogy may seem crude and overstated, but it explains much of what is happening in congregational and community life. Churches feel under pressure to do those things in worship and in other programs which will cause them to be attractive to people who are "shopping" for a church home. When people become dissatisfied with what is happening in a congregation, they are considerably more likely than past generations to simply change to another church.

- The transition across society to a lower level of trust in large institutions and persons who are beyond local control. Public confidence in politicians and government agencies continues to be at a very low level. Likewise, people have more difficulty trusting denominational leaders and organizations beyond the level of the local church. Lacking personal interactions with those persons and agencies, local church members often feel uncomfortable trusting large sums of money to denominational projects.

- The transition to more informal styles of worship. Vast numbers of churches around the country experience tension between newer and older members of the congregation over the style of worship. What is done with contemporary music? Do drama and video replace the sermon at least part of the time? Are shorts, jeans, and sport shirts appropriate attire for worship? The pastor whose church is growing without significant tension over such issues is fortunate indeed. Most churches which are growing must continuously balance the desire of older, life-long members for very

traditional worship with the desire of prospective members and newer members for more contemporary services. Some congregations handle this by compromise within existing services; others add options.

- The transition in society which is resulting in large numbers of people working at jobs which do not support a high standard of living. Many of the new positions created over the last two decades have been at or just slightly above the minimum wage level. Consider what happened to the median income in this country when looked at in constant 1994 dollars between 1989 and 1994:

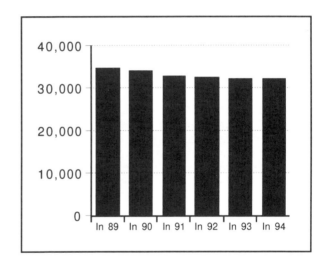

[The above information comes from **The Statistical Abstract of the United States.**]

The real purchasing power at the median income level actually went down somewhat between 1989 and 1994. The median income level is the exact mid-point. Half the incomes are higher, and half are lower. Those of us who live well above the median level often fail to recognize the magnitude of the pressures on those below that level.

The new jobs which pay well are ones which require significant amounts of education. College education has become increasingly expensive, and considerable financial aid has moved from scholarships and grants to loans. More and more students are graduating from college with large debt loads. All these factors affect how people feel about giving to the church.

- There is a transition for many people from a personal faith nurtured by the church to one which is nurtured in more private ways. The lack of confidence in established religious organizations by many people in our society is not paralleled by a lack of interest in spiritual concerns. In many respects, we actually seem to be in a time of spiritual awakening or at least of heightened interest in spiritual matters. That awakening, however, is more focused on individualized religion than on traditional religious organizations.

  In certain respects, the very lack of confidence in the institutions of society may be causing some persons to search with greater intentionality for knowledge and experiences which transcend those institutions. As this book goes to press, we are seeing continued interest in television shows like *Touched by an Angel* and *Promised Land* which are focused on religious issues.

  The spiritual searching of people, both inside and outside of the institutional church, however, has not for the most part been related to what people do with their financial resources. That connection must be made both for the health of our religious institutions and also for the spiritual well-being of those seeking to grow closer to God.

The Christian Community Spirituality and Giving Project

Christian Community, which is the publisher of this report and the sponsor of the study on which it is based, is a nonprofit organization focused on research and development to assist local congregations in their ministries to pressing needs in church and society. The range of concerns of the organization has been broad and currently includes:

- Work on church growth and vitality, including approaches to faith-sharing. We are especially concerned about ways to help active church members comfortably talk about their faith without using canned formulas or tactics which feel manipulative to them. We are also concerned that the outreach of our churches be broad enough to incorporate people who are different than those already active in our congregations.

- Creation of models to help churches become more directly involved in community development and in the provision of new opportunities to persons who are in need – building on their assets rather than focusing on their deficiencies. We are concerned about the extent to which our society as a whole, including many churches, has begun to view the poor in negative, sometimes judgmental ways.

- Development of resources and of programs to help teenagers and young adults develop more positively assertive styles. We are concerned about the tendency of some young people, most frequently males, to become aggressive and violent in frustration over failure to achieve their desires in more positive ways. We are likewise concerned about the tendency of others, most frequently females, to be so nonassertive as to become victims. Churches have a unique opportunity to help young people develop positive self-images, grounded in Christ, which prevent them from being aggressors or victims and empower them to change society for the better.

- Strategic planning with local churches wanting to more precisely focus their work and move into the future with confidence. That process sometimes includes working through divisions and problems which have become barriers to the congregation moving into the future.

This brief background is shared so that you will understand that the interests and concerns of Christian Community are broader than the study which is the focus of this publication. Those broader interests and commitments, Christian Community believes, have a positive impact on the approach which has been taken to the Spirituality and Giving Project and to the resulting development of resources.

As we conducted national studies on church growth and decline and as we worked with specific local congregations in strategic planning in the early nineteen-nineties, we increasingly became aware of the extent to which stewardship problems were beginning to affect local congregations. We have been well acquainted with many excellent stewardship resources published by others and of many excellent Christian fund-raisers, and we have frequently referred people to those resources and services. As we encountered more and more congregations struggling with steward-ship issues, however, we developed a desire to better understand what was happening from a research perspective.

We received cooperation from over eleven hundred local congregations in looking at figures, trends, practices, and theologies of stewardship. We were especially interested in identifying those practices and trends which consistently resulted in increased giving without being manipulative or unethical – and in identifying those practices which seemed to be harmful to the development of a positive sense of stewardship in the congregation.

We had the cooperation of local congregations of the following denominations or traditions in the study:

- United Methodist
- Disciples of Christ (Christian Church)
- Presbyterian Church, U.S.A.
- United Church of Christ
- Episcopal
- Evangelical Lutheran
- American Baptist
- Southern Baptist
- Missouri Synod Lutheran
- Roman Catholic
- Church of the Brethren
- Mennonite
- Assemblies of God
- Unitarian Church

- Reformed
- Evangelical Covenant
- Brethren Church (Ashland, Ohio)
- Wesleyan
- Moravian
- Free Methodist
- Church of God
- Evangelical Free Church
- Nazarene

We also received cooperation from several churches not affiliated with any mainline or evangelical denomination.

We found, as have many others who studied stewardship concerns, that the differences among the denominations in regard to stewardship were not so striking as the differences among individual congrega-tions. For the most part, practices which are effective in one denomination are effective in another. Practices which are harmful in one denomination are just as likely to be harmful in another.

There are differences between Roman Catholic parishes and Protestant churches which should be noted. The differences which we found are similar to those which have been observed by others. Larger Catholic parishes seem to need proportionately less money to operate than smaller Protestant churches. There are some economies of scale, and the compensation and benefits to priests are generally less than to Protestant clergy. Catholic priests in general seem more reluctant than Protestant clergy to talk about money and to push for higher giving. Many Catholic dioceses, however, are using very sophisticated direct solicitation techniques to gain support for their programs and missions.

Some differences of opinion exists among researchers about the extent to which Catholic dissatisfaction with the official church position on birth control and other issues may contribute to decreased giving. Certainly many Protestant churches have also been impacted by unhappiness about denominational positions on various issues, especially on homosexuality and abortion. Within Protestant churches, we found evidence that strong feelings over such issues are more likely to impact the willingness of people to support the denominational level than to support the local congregation. It's very difficult to construct a study which adequately weighs the number of variables involved.

Many Catholic parishes, like Protestant churches, are going through a period of careful examination of their stewardship programs and are seeking improved ways to do stewardship education. [For more discussion and comparison of giving between Roman Catholics and Protestants, see Dean Hoge's insightful book *Money Matters: Personal Giving in American Churches*, Westminster John Knox, 1996. Also see Andrew Greeley's thought-provoking book *Religious Change in America*, Harvard University Press, 1989.]

A Spiritual Issue

Christian Community felt before doing this study and feels even more so after the study that financial giving is a spiritual issue. The motivations which are healthiest and which are most effective are those which grow out of the individual's relationship with God and with the rest of the Christian community. In fact we are thoroughly convinced that most people in our churches want to improve their levels of giving to the local congregation and to other worthy programs and missions. For the most part, stewardship education is not burdened with the task for getting people to do something to which they are opposed.

When we began working with congregations to test strategies for improved giving, we found that many people liked the theme *The Desires of Your Heart*. The words come from Psalm 37, which is not one of the more commonly used stewardship passages in the Bible. The Psalm as a whole speaks of patience and trust in God. Verses 4-6 read:

> *Trust in the LORD, and do good;*
> *so you will live in the land,*
> *and enjoy security.*
>
> *Take delight in the LORD,*
> *and he will give you the*
> *desires of your heart.*
>
> *Commit your way to the LORD;*
> *trust in him, and he will act.*

> *He will make your vindication*
> *shine like the light,*
> *and the justice of your cause*
> *like the noonday.*

The deepest desires of the hearts of people are not for fame, wealth, and power. The deepest desires of people are for closer relationships with God and with one another, for lives that are meaningful, and for the sense that they are making a difference in the world. While people may live as though more superficial desires are the top priorities in their lives, there is a level at which they are very much aware of what is truly important. Our surveys and our work with local congregations convince us of that truth. In fact the words of our Lord which are printed around the heart-logo on the cover of this book convey well the best desires of the heart for each of us [Luke 10:27]:

> *You shall love the LORD your God*
> *with all your heart,*
> *and with all your soul,*
> *and with all your strength,*
> *and with all your mind;*
> *and your neighbor as yourself.*

Effective stewardship programs help people connect with the deepest desires of their hearts and grow in their relationships with Jesus Christ. Effective stewardship programs, however, do have to include some talk about money!

And as the three pastors observed during the breakfast meeting described at the start of this chapter, it's no easy matter to get people to talk about money in the church. And if we don't get people to talk about money and think about money, stewardship does not improve. How to do that effectively is one of the major themes of this report.

The authors of this report are thoroughly convinced that there are specific steps which every congregation can take which will result in improved giving. These are steps which are not manipulative, and they are steps which, in fact, help people deepen their spiritual lives.

What Motivates Giving To the Church?

"When we did a capital funds drive for our building expansion," Frank shared with Teresa at another breakfast meeting (which Jim had to miss), "the consultant we hired told us to be sure to select people for visits who were liked and respected by the people they would be talking with about giving. He told us to be especially careful who made the approaches for the largest gifts. 'Who asks who,' he used to say, 'is the crucial question.' People give in order to look good to others, and they don't want to lose the respect of others."

"I've heard that too," said Teresa. "That's the way we structure things when we do fund-raising for the Philharmonic. Of course there we actually print the categories in which people give. Over five thousand; two to five thousand; one to two thousand; five hundred to a thousand; two-fifty to five hundred; one hundred to two-fifty; and under a hundred. I know that approach works, but I also have a problem with it. It feels like people are simply giving in order to get credit for it. By printing the names in categories by amount, we're also exercising a subtle form of blackmail on people who are especially concerned about how they look. It might work, but I'm glad we don't do it in the church."

"I think what you can do in the church depends a lot on the customs of the congre-gation," Frank responded. "When I pastored my last African-American congregation, we routinely printed the names of all the tithers. Then we decided that was causing others in the church to feel uncomfortable, so we stopped doing it. When we stopped printing the names, at least a third of the people stopped tithing. We went back to printing them."

"But you don't do that in the church you're pastoring now, do you?" Teresa asked.

"No way. I'm so far over in the land of white people that my skin has lightened a shade." Teresa and Frank both laughed. Frank is African American. "No one would take printing a list of tithers in my congre-gation today. The best we can do to influence people is to pay attention to who does the solicitation for big gifts."

"When I think about the largest givers in my home congregation, I'm struck by the fact that several of them are very self-effacing and don't appear to want credit for what they are doing. These are people who really under-stand the spiritual dimension of giving. They give because they want to in response to what God has done for them."

"Thank God for those folks," agreed Frank. "We have them too. Part of what makes me uneasy is that most of them are older members of the church. Many of our younger members don't give for the same reasons."

"Some of the younger members in my church give out of a sense of obligation, to pay for the programs and services that they want," Teresa said. "Then there are those who give because they want to make a difference. That's part of our problem. We have people who'll dig deep in their pockets for a special cause, but the same people aren't excited about supporting the general budget of the church."

"I had a widower who gave the church $15,000 a year," Frank shared. "He died, and the whole estate went to his daughter. The total pledges of the last ten new members we received into the church don't add up to $15,000. Losing one person like that has a big impact on the budget."

"It's a shame he didn't remember your

church in his will," Teresa observed.

"I agree. On the other hand, we need to change the stewardship patterns of our younger members."

"But no one can give $15,000 a year unless that person has a substantial income. If that's a tithe, it means $150,000 a year. My church only has a couple of people who earn at that level."

"With the exception of a couple of physicians, the younger members of my church don't earn that much either," Frank said. "The gentleman who died was very comfortable, but he actually did more than tithe. I think his total retirement income was around $60,000. He simply chose to give a fourth of it to the church. That's real commitment."

"Then I think of an elderly woman in my congregation who is very open about her income and her giving; she tries to be a positive influence on others," Teresa shared. "She gives the church $2,000 a year and has a retirement income of $16,000. That represents real sacrifice for her. $16,000 isn't much to live on today."

"It sure isn't. Tithing may not be a realistic goal for some people. Still, the people who do tithe always seem to be all right."

"There are some economic laws at work in the world that economists and stock brokers haven't figured out."

Looking at Motivation

Teresa and Frank are certainly right when they say that there are economic laws which are not normally considered by economists and stock brokers. From the standpoint of financial planning and making the most of resources, in fact, it makes little sense to give anything substantial to the church or any other charitable organization!

Yet the reality is that people give generously to many charitable causes, including the church. The range of motivations for giving is broad and may differ significantly from person to person. People give to the church and other charitable organizations because:

- They are responding with thankfulness for God's generosity, for all they have received.

- They understand the Christian concept of stewardship and see themselves as custodians of resources which in fact belong to God.

- They feel a Christian obligation to support the church. They may feel that tithing (10% of one's income) is the standard for giving to the church.

- They feel part of the church or part of another charitable organization and therefore feel good about supporting its work.

- They identify with the needs of the people being served and feel moved to help them.

- They feel guilty over what they have accumulated or over things they have done, and giving to the church and other charitable causes helps them feel better about themselves.

- They want to look good in the eyes of others and give generously for that reason.

- They respect others who give generously and model their own giving after those persons.

- They are asked to give by someone to whom they feel an obligation.

- They have a strong desire to make a difference in the church or in the world, and they see financial giving as one way to accomplish that.

- They believe that when they give generously to the church and to other causes that God in fact blesses their lives, perhaps in financial ways but often in other ways.

- Giving generously helps them feel closer to God and better about themselves.

- They give out of discipline or habit. Having grown up sharing their resources with the church and with other charitable causes, they simply consider that an integral part of their identity.

- They give because they are emotionally moved by the manner in which the appeal is made.

- They give because they feel they are benefiting from the programs and services of the church or other organization, and they feel an obligation to help support those programs and services.

And the list could be continued for pages! For most of us, giving is not a matter of responding to a single motivation but more often to a cluster of motivations. The motivations which are strongest generally control the extent of our generosity. Obviously those who give primarily in support of programs and services are not likely to be as generous as those who give out of a deep sense of Christian stewardship.

Before exploring more fully what we learned about motivation in the Spirituality and Giving Project, let's take a brief look at the project itself.

The Spirituality and Giving Project

While the details of a research project are not of interest to most readers, some basic background information generally is helpful. If the churches studied are almost all of a different denominational tradition than your own congregation and almost all of a size very different than your own, then you understandably might feel skeptical about the significance of the results for your particular congregation.

As shared in the first chapter, we had the cooperation of more than eleven hundred congregations, 1157 to be exact. In order to gain the cooperation of those 1157 congregations, we made initial contact by letter with 4,974 congregations. That means that 23.3% of the congregations contacted agreed to share in our study. That's, in fact, a higher percentage than we anticipated. At a

minimum, we asked leadership in participating churches to complete a very substantial survey and to send us considerable information on church finances. That itself was a time-consuming task. We also asked people to be available for phone interviews, which were conducted with leaders of over fifty congregations; and we asked another fifty churches to distribute surveys to the entire membership. Over a hundred congregations, in a variety of ways, later worked with us as we experimented to see the impact of various changes on levels of giving.

Most of the participating congregations can best be described as "mainline Protestant," although there are also Roman Catholic parishes and more evangelical congregations. There are also several Anabaptist congregations (Brethren Church, Church of the Brethren, and Mennonite) and several Unitarian congregations. Here are the numbers by denominational category:

United Methodist	104
Disciples of Christ (Christian Church)	102
Presbyterian, U.S.A.	102
United Church of Christ	101
Episcopal	72
Evangelical Lutheran	68
American Baptist	65
Southern Baptist	53
Independent Churches	52
Missouri Synod Lutheran	45
Roman Catholic	44
Church of the Brethren	42
Mennonite	41
Assemblies of God	40
Unitarian Church	40
Reformed	25
Evangelical Covenant	22
Brethren Church (Ashland, Ohio)	19
Wesleyan	18
Moravian	18
Free Methodist	17
Church of God	16
Evangelical Free Church	15
Nazarene	15
Other	21
Total	1,157

The congregations represented a good mix of rural, suburban, and urban settings. A few of the Mennonite congregations are located in Canada, but the rest are in the United States.

Forty-five of the fifty states are represented. We later conducted thirty phone interviews with leaders in Canadian churches in an attempt to better understand the similarities and differences between Canada and the United States.

Only twenty-seven of the congregations were of predominantly African American, Korean, or other ethnic minority composition. A separate study was conducted involving fifty-eight churches in the African Methodist Episcopal Church and in the African Methodist Episcopal Zion Church. The methodology used was sufficiently different that those churches are not included in the statistical information in this report.

The participating churches represented a broad range of size in terms of official membership, average worship attendance, and budget. The churches by official membership:

Under 50	84
51 - 100	98
101 - 250	201
251 - 400	253
401 - 600	157
601 - 1,000	101
1,000 - 2,500	109
Over 2500	154
Total	1,157

Estimates of membership were made for those parishes which record members in family units rather than by individuals.

In evaluating the results of a study such as the Spirituality and Giving Project, one might well ask the question: "How are the churches which participated different from those which did not?" There is no way to answer that question with certainty. Our assumption, however, is that church leaders who chose to participate in the study had a higher than normal desire to deal in a forthright way with stewardship issues. If they did not have that desire, they would have been unlikely to complete such lengthy questionnaires and to participate in other ways. Thus the churches and the congregational leaders who shared in the Spirituality and Giving Project may well be ahead of many other congregations in dealing with stewardship concerns.

As shared in the first chapter, we did not find many differences by denomination, with the exception of differences between Roman Catholic parishes and Protestant churches. In this report, we'll refer to differences when relevant; but for the most part what was true for one denomination was true for others.

Age and Giving

The study asked church leaders for their opinions concerning the relationship between age and giving.

Half or more of the church's budget is supported by the giving of persons 60 years of age and older. **45.6%** agreed

Young adults in the congregation seem less willing or able than older adults to support the church through regular pledging and giving to the budget. **63.4%** agreed

It seems to me that the donor base for our church is getting smaller and older. **49.9%** agreed

Respondents were also asked to indicate whether or not the adult membership of the church roughly reflected the age distribution in the community. **Seventy percent** (70.18%) indicated that it did not. In most instances, the adult membership of the church was older than the norm in the community.

Clearly, large numbers of congregations are very dependent on older members to meet the financial needs of the church. Pastors, church treasurers, and financial secretaries indicated in written comments and in interviews that all of these factors are frequently true:

- Younger members are not being added as quickly as older members are retiring and dying.

- Younger members are less likely than older members to have developed the habit of tithing or proportionate giving.

- Young adults in the church generally do not have the same financial resources as older adults. Thus they cannot give as much even if they are motivated to give generously from what they have.

It's also clear both from the comments of those completing the lengthier congregational questionnaires and from the survey responses of individual church members that the motivations for giving do show some age-level differences. In response to surveys taken by congregational members, adults over the age of sixty were far more likely than adults between the ages of eighteen and thirty-five to agree with these statements:

- "I tithe my income to the church (give at least 10%)."

- "I have given money to the church when it was a personal sacrifice to do so."

- "The main reason I give to the church is because of my commitment to Christ."

- "The main reason I give to the church is out of gratitude to God."

Young adults were far more likely to express agreement with statements like these:

- "I cannot afford to give a tithe (10% of my income) to the church."

- "An important reason for giving money to the church is to support the services and programs I utilize."

- "I increasingly feel unwilling to see my money used outside of our local congregation unless I know what that money will do."

- "I do not have adequate knowledge of the good done by our church through funds sent to the denomination."

Leaders who completed the full congregational questionnaire were in strong agreement with these statements:

Most church members today are more focused on what they can get out of the church (a consumer view) than on what service they can give through the church. **77.2%** agreed

Many church members today see giving to the church as payment or reimbursement for services rather than as gifts to God. **72.9%** agreed

Those completing the full congregational questionnaire were asked to rank ten factors in order of importance in motivating giving in their congregations. Here are the percentages which placed each item as the number one motivator in their congregation:

Commitment to Christ	43.4%
Desire to support the church's program	20.1%
Belief that giving is a spiritual matter and that generous giving benefits one's spiritual life	9.1%
Identification with the people supported by the church's ministries	7.5%
Discipline or habit developed over the years	6.6%
Desire to make a difference in the world	3.5%
Other	3.2%
Respect and appreciation for the pastor and/or other staff	2.5%
Guilt	1.8%
Conviction that tithing is important	0.17%

(Note: Tithing or proportionate giving received much greater importance in second and third place rankings.)

When congregational members were asked to rank the same items which had been ranked by their leaders, some age level differences clearly emerged. Among young adults (18-35 years of age), the desire to support the church's program was given a number one ranking almost as often as commitment to Christ. Young adults were also considerably more likely than older adults to give weight to their appreciation for the pastor and/or other staff members when determining what they would give to the church.

It's clear that age level differences need to be taken into consideration in designing our stewardship approaches with our congregations. As this report continues, you'll find that stewardship education is a major emphasis. People's reasons for giving do not change without exposure to new information.

Talking about Money

But stewardship education means talking about money, and most of our congregations are less than enthusiastic about that topic! Very few of the congregations participating in the study had systematic programs of stewardship education which involved children, youth, and adults during the year.

Congregational members who completed individual surveys also made it clear that money is not a popular topic of conversation. People feel uncomfortable about the idea of talking about money. Pastors feel they will be subjected to criticism for dwelling too much on financial matters in sermons and in other settings.

Yet one of our significant learnings from the Spirituality and Giving Project is that people feel more uncomfortable about the *idea* of talking about money than they do when actually talking about it. The anticipation of dealing with the topic is more uncomfortable than actually dealing with it.

In fact we found that churches which have moved ahead with stewardship education have lower numbers of people unhappy about talking about money than churches which have done very little stewardship education. Churches which move ahead with stewardship education find that the results are overwhelmingly positive.

There are some basics which are crucial when it comes to dealing with people and money in the church. It's very important that:

- People feel their confidentiality is honored by the church, and that they not feel put on the spot to talk with a group of people about the actual amount of their giving. Talking about the concept of giving is another matter entirely.

- People feel that their giving, at whatever level, is appreciated – that they never feel "put down" for not giving more than they currently are.

- People not feel that their level of giving has any relationship to the availability of pastoral care to them or to the quality of the concern of the congregation for them.

As long as basics such as these are honored, people in fact can respond very positively to more conversation about stewardship. They especially respond positively when a direct connection is made between stewardship and the spiritual life. They also respond positively as they are helped to see the kind of difference which their giving through the church makes in the life of the congregation and in the lives of individuals.

In all fifty of the congregations which distributed surveys to the entire membership, we found that **over 75% of the members completing the surveys would like to be doing more for the church financially!** The best desires of the hearts of people include the wish to give more generously. We also found that **over 78% of the members completing the surveys said that they would benefit from more opportunity to understand and discuss the spiritual significance of money in their lives and in society.** Yet it's also true that about the same percentage said that they find it initially difficult or uncomfortable to talk about money in the church. We need to find comfortable ways to help people talk about this important area of the spiritual life.

With this as background, let's proceed to examine what we have identified as the top ten ways to improve giving in the congregation.

The Top Ten Ways To Increase Giving In Your Congregation

Most of the material in this report is organized around the ten overall strategies which the Spirituality and Giving Project has identified as being the most effective ways to increase giving in your congregation. The very fact that you purchased this report and are studying this material suggests that you are more fully understanding of financial dynamics in the congregation than many others, and that you are no doubt already implementing some of these strategies.

Our study has convinced us that the more these strategies are implemented in the church, the more significant the increase in giving will be. If your congregation is not currently implementing several of these strategies, however, don't try to start them all at once. Choose the ones which appear most appropriate for your current situation and start with them. Develop a plan to continue adding strategies over the next few years.

As you read the pages which follow, think about other persons and groups in your church who could benefit from studying this material:

- The Memorials Committee or the Bequests Committee.

- The pastor and other church staff.

- The Personnel Committee or the Pastor-Staff Relations Committee.

- The treasurer and the church financial secretary.

- Any groups involved in helping promote special offerings.

- The education or nurture commission which should be involved in efforts to improve stewardship education.

- The missions commission or whatever group has the primary responsibility for interpreting and promoting the mission outreach of the congregation.

- The administrative board, church board, or other top organizational structure in your congregation. Since effective stewardship education will at some points involve all leadership groups in the church, it's very helpful to have the top administrative group aware of the most effective approaches.

- And of course the finance or stewardship committee or commission of your church. That group may wish to set up a schedule to study all of this material and together identify beneficial changes for your congregation.

1. *Connect individual giving directly to the spiritual life of each person.*

2. *Begin practicing stewardship education as a twelve-month process which involves children, youth, and adults.*

3. *Encourage tithing or proportionate giving.*

4. *Let people make pledges and regular gifts to more than a single fund, encouraging rather than discouraging designated giving.*

5. *Provide opportunity for people to give from both checking and savings.*

6. *Promote special offerings more effectively.*

7. *Encourage the pastor to be actively involved in stewardship education and fund-raising.*

8. *Send more frequent financial statements to members and constituents who support the church.*

9. *Emphasize the mission and vision of your church rather than the line item budget — and remember that people give to people and God, not budgets.*

10. *Help people give through their wills, living trusts, life insurance policies, and similar means.*

1. Connect individual giving directly to the spiritual life of each person.

"God has blessed my life, and it just seems right for me to return some of that through the church," said Mike in a cottage meeting for the church's annual financial campaign. "As generous as the Lord has been to me, I need to be generous to others."

"We're all at different places in life, and that affects what we can give," said Alice. "I know Mike has been generous to the church. Of course I don't know how generous, but I do know he paid for the organ repair last year, and that was no small thing. But my husband and I have a son in college and a daughter who will be in college next year. There's a limit to how much we can do."

Alice continued: "We used to not give much to the church. Then we felt challenged when Pastor Wagner told us that he and his wife gave ten percent. We started talking and realized that the Pastor and his wife probably earned about the same thing that we did and that they also had two kids headed for college. We didn't come up to a full tithe, but we're giving a lot better now – and I feel like we've been blessed for doing it. Our spiritual lives are fuller and richer because we're taking our giving more seriously. We aren't to a tithe yet, but I think we'll get there."

The Spiritual Life and Giving

Over 43% of the church leaders we surveyed feel that commitment to Christ is the top motivating factor in high levels of giving in their congregations. In the fifty congregations which invited every member to complete a survey, we found that among those who tithed, over 80% said that commitment to Christ and a response to God's blessings were the main reasons for doing so. These are people with a strong feeling of thankfulness to God for the blessings of life. People who feel good about life, good about the blessings they've received, and good about their relationships with Christ want to give generously when given appropriate opportunities.

Our work makes clear that the persons who give at the highest levels do not do so out of guilt or obligation. They do so because of thankful hearts and close relationships with Christ and with others in the church. The reality is, however, that many people in our congregations have not been helped to think through a proper response to God's blessings.

In some ways, many of us have lost touch with our own historical roots. In *Behind the Stained Glass Windows*, John and Sylvia Ronsvalle quote these words from Craig Dykstra, vice president of the Lilly Endowment, Inc.: "The Lutheran view of giving as thanksgiving for grace or the Calvinist perspective of managing possessions that ultimately are not our own or the Wesleyan position that giving is part of the perfecting work of God – these historic understandings are not widely known any more."

In too many instances, because of our discomfort in dealing with the topic of money and giving in the church, we've settled for financial campaigns which were more focused on raising the budget than on helping people deepen their spiritual lives.

Our efforts at raising necessary funds for the church need to center more on the connection of giving to the spiritual life. This reality has several implications for raising funds and for stewardship education:

- Appeal primarily to people's commitment to Christ, to their sense of thanksgiving, and to their connections with others in the body of Christ.

- When talking about the needs of the church, do so primarily in terms of mission and vision as part of the body of Christ rather than in terms of budget line items.

- When focusing on a particular need or cause such as building renovation or an additional staff member, point out the benefits to the spiritual life of the congregation or to the need to reach out in Christ's name.

- Remember that building a clear connection between the spiritual life and giving can't be accomplished in a single financial campaign. Year-round stewardship education is crucial.

Kennon Callahan, in *Effective Church Finances*, writes: "The purpose of a giving campaign is to help people grow forward the generosity of their giving, not to raise a detailed line-item budget. It is not necessary – indeed, it is not always useful – to have the total budget decided completely and exactly before having a giving campaign" [p.5].

Viewing oneself as a steward requires a mature faith. The Greek word for steward is *oikonomos*, which is derived from another Greek word, *oikos*, literally meaning "residence." The Greek *oikoumene* referred to the whole world or the inhabited earth. Everyone in a residence has an intimate responsibility for the others who live there. A steward is a manager, custodian, or trustee for something owned by someone else.

We aren't accustomed to thinking of ourselves as anything other than the owners of what we possess. Teaching about stewardship is important, but it isn't always the most effective way to motivate persons whose own faith is not yet mature. A person or household taking stewardship seriously will give out of commitment, but many people give more generously out of compassion for the needs of others. The giving strategies of the church must continually work to build the spiritual maturity of people in a way that appreciates their role as stewards, but those strategies must also help people who are at a different point in their faith development connect in meaningful ways to the needs of

people, their sense of belonging to the congregation, and other points of identity.

This offertory prayer appears occasionally in journals of humor and in stewardship materials:

> *O God, no matter what we say or do,*
> *Here is what we really think of you.*
> *Amen*

The prayer has surfaced in so many circles that we don't know with whom to credit it! We don't recommend your use of the prayer at morning worship, but it does convey an interesting and potentially important truth – what we do with our financial resources is a very clear indicator of how deep our connection with God really is, as well as how mature we are in the spiritual life.

Estimates of the percentage of verses in Matthew, Mark, and Luke which deal with financial matters run as high as one-sixth. Sixteen of the parables of Jesus concern stewardship and material resources. What we do with our material goods relates very directly to how close we grow to God. When people feel close to God and see their money and other assets as gifts from God to be used to further God's kingdom, they may give even more generously than we expect. In 2 Corinthians, Paul wrote:

> *For, as I can testify, they voluntarily*
> *gave according to their means, and*
> *even beyond their means, begging*
> *us earnestly for the privilege of sharing*
> *in this ministry to the saints – and*
> *this, not merely as we expected; they*
> *gave themselves first to the LORD,*
> *and by the will of God, to us, so*
> *that we might urge Titus that, as he*
> *had already made a beginning,*
> *so he should also complete this*
> *generous undertaking among you* [8:3-7].

People do have a true spirit of generosity, and they are continually pulled to the heart of God. Whether they are spiritually mature or immature, God is continually seeking to be at work in their lives. The result of this is that positive approaches to increase giving within the church almost always work better than negative ones.

When we solicit gifts for ministry in an

apologetic way, we fail to take advantage of the natural connectedness of people with God. The president of a primarily African-American, church-related college once said: "I'm excited about the difference my college makes in the lives of young people. I'm excited about the way God has enabled us to take students who barely qualified to start college and then turn them into teachers and social workers and doctors and dentists. And I think there is almost nothing finer that a Christian can do with his or her money than use it to provide scholarships to turn around the lives of these young people. . . . I'm *never* apologetic when I ask for money. I'm sharing an opportunity. They have to decide how to respond. . . . I also accept it when they say 'no.' Overall, I am absolutely convinced that I do as much for the donor as for the recipient. I connect the donor to something greater than himself or herself, and God pulls us all toward that kind of relationship."

Our individual and group approaches to asking others to give work best when we:

1. Are personally excited about the cause – enough so that we consider it a privilege to support that cause ourselves and are absolutely unapologetic about giving others opportunity to support that cause.

2. Remember that very few people resent being asked to support an important cause. They simply want us to respect the genuine limits which may exist for them.

   When we asked individual members of congregations to complete surveys, we found repeatedly that people did not mind requests for funds for a wide range of causes in the church – so long as they felt free to say "yes" or "no" each time without guilt or pressure.

3. Remember that people like to be thanked for what they have given. Both as individuals seeking support for the church and its ministries and as groups or organizations within the church, we need to be generous in our expressions of thanks and appreciation for the gifts which people make.

Though God is continually pulling us all

into closer relationship, people differ in the extent to which they have deepened the spiritual life. The same strategies will not have the same impact on all individuals in the church. Stewardship education needs to happen throughout the year.

Approaches to the Annual Campaign

For most churches, however, there is no getting away from an annual giving campaign in which people are encouraged to make pledges or statements of intention of giving for the entire year. If a large percentage of the congregation had a mature faith, then annual giving campaigns might not be needed. At the present state of development in most churches, those campaigns are important; they often result in twice as much support for the church than if no campaign was held.

The focus of what you want to accomplish in your campaign may differ from one year to the next. You can push for major increases in congregational giving perhaps every three or four years. The campaigns in between those major pushes need to be somewhat less forceful and work at developing things such as:

- Increasing the number of persons working in the area of stewardship and finance.

- Increasing the percentage of house-holds who support the church.

- Increasing the number of persons who tithe.

- Increasing the number of persons who have opportunity to help set the priorities for the ministry of the congregation.

- Increasing the number of persons who receive at least some stewardship education.

And every campaign needs to work at deepening the spiritual life of members of the congregation. Such efforts during a campaign should not, however, be seen as a substitute for other stewardship education efforts during the year.

Consider the strengths and weaknesses of the major options for financial campaigns which are being used in the United States and Canada:

1. **Cottage Meetings** (small group meetings held in homes) or other small group approaches are an underutilized strategy in most of our churches. Only 9% of the congregations we surveyed had used cottage meetings or small groups as the primary basis for a financial campaign in the last three years. Cottage meetings, however, provide an ideal opportunity to encourage people to talk together about the spiritual life and about the needs of the congregation.

The weakness of this approach is that cottage meetings or a similar small group strategy will not generally reach many people who are not already supporting the church. Like many other church programs, those you would most like to attend will stay away! They will help people who are currently supporting the church better relate their giving to the spiritual life and think about how much of an increase should be possible.

2. **Celebration Sunday** approaches involve the least pressure and, as generally implemented, the least work of the major strategies being utilized. These are sometimes called Consecration Sunday, Pledge Sunday, or Commitment Sunday. Over 40% of the congregations we surveyed had used such an approach at least once in the last three years. Efforts are all focused on a single Sunday at which time members turn in their intention of giving or pledge cards at a special dinner or on the altar of the church. The steps leading up to that Sunday help involve large numbers of members, and the best plans include a special effort to reach persons who are not normally active in the church.

This strategy can be a good change of pace, and the results may be good if the steps suggested are all followed. This strategy will often not be as effective as cottage meetings at raising the level of giving by individual people, because it generally does not stimulate as much conversation about giving and the spiritual life.

Though in general we are refraining from commenting about specific campaign materials except for our own, we do want to say that we have encountered extremely high levels of satisfaction from congregations using Herb Miller's *Consecration Sunday* approach [available from Cokesbury as of this writing]. Miller's materials have been broadly used over the years, and we did not encounter any congregation dissatisfied with them except for a couple who did not follow the very precise instructions! *Consecration Sunday* does involve more work than most other Celebration Sunday approaches.

3. **Pass-It-On** approaches involve people in delivering pledge materials and other financial information on a door-to-door basis. The congregation is generally divided into circuits or neighborhoods of six to fifteen households, and the materials are passed from household to household. Each family or individual removes pledge materials and information, completes a pledge and seals it in the envelope, and then passes the materials to the next home.

These approaches are sometimes called Pony Express, Saddlebag, or Circuit Rider; and the materials available for these from commercial and nonprofit sources are generally of high quality. The strategy is sufficiently common that many churches simply design their own. Almost thirty percent of the churches we surveyed have used such an approach at least once in the last three years.

This approach does a good job increasing the number of giving units and involving people. In fact, when properly utilized, it effectively touches every household in the congregation except for those which are located at a great distance from the community (and provisions can of course be made to reach those persons by mail and phone during any financial campaign). This approach won't necessarily motivate people to make significant increases in their own levels of giving, because the educational aspect comes primarily through what people read and what they hear about in worship or classes at church.

We did find that some churches have overworked this approach by using it year-after-year-after-year. While any approach can obviously be overworked, it appears especially easy to do so with this one. After a couple of years in succession, the fun of passing the saddlebags, pass-it-on bag, or other material from house to house has worn off. We did find that people responded especially positively to approaches in this category in which people were invited to share a small gift with the household to which they took the pledge materials. Some people baked bread or cookies; some gave flowers or small plants; and some gave devotional materials.

4. **An Every Member Visitation** will generally provide the best overall means for raising the level of giving and also for increasing the number of giving units in the congregation. But this one is a major effort and requires a great deal of work, starting far in advance.

In an every member visitation, trained teams of people make visits to each household to explain the needs of the church and to solicit the support of those who are visited. Visitors are often encouraged to witness to their own giving – not always sharing the precise dollars they give but sharing the percentage of their incomes which they give and the reasons for their giving.

When the visitors are properly trained, an every member visitation provides a marvelous opportunity for stewardship education. We found church leaders generally reluctant to conduct an every member visitation, but the responses from those who did so were nearly always excellent. When the training is properly done and the visitors become comfortable discussing stewardship, those who are visited do not feel uncomfortable talking about money.

About nine percent of the churches we surveyed had used an every member visitation sometime in the three years preceding the survey date. Over half of those congregations had done so in connection with a building campaign or major capital campaign rather than simply to increase the overall stewardship of the congregation.

The main barriers we found to every member visitations were the substantial amount of advanced planning required, the large number of volunteers needed, and the demands of other church programs for both volunteers and meeting dates.

In connection with an every member visitation, those who receive training to visit, and sometimes those who are especially high givers, may be invited to a special dinner for a motivational talk and are invited to make their own pledges at that time. This can lower the total number of visits which must be made, and the results are generally very positive. (An advanced gifts dinner can also be integrated into the other giving campaign approaches.)

In spite of all the work involved, an every member visitation remains the approach which is most likely to result in significant increases in the level of giving in a congregation. It is also an approach which misses only those persons who are living outside the local area (and thus must be reached by mail or by phone) and those persons who adamantly refuse to accept a visit (which is generally a very small number of households).

Cautions about Campaigns

Herb Mather, in his thought-provoking book *Don't Shoot the Horse ('Til You Know How to Drive the Tractor)*, points out that we put too much confidence in campaigns. These are painful words for an organization such as ours which has developed a new giving campaign manual (a separate publication):

> *Campaign methods, manuals, and materials are vastly overrated. Their effectiveness is especially inflated by people who are trying to sell them* [p. 18].

But our research confirms the truth of his statement! That's why we so strongly advocate not only variety in the means used for the annual campaign but also an intentional move to increasing opportunities for stewardship education and raised giving throughout the year.

Obviously there are many different ways to combine elements from the different campaign approaches which we've described here. You can use a Pass It On approach in combination with a Celebration Sunday. You can use Cottage Meetings in combination with a Celebration Sunday. You can use Cottage Meetings as part of an Every Member Visitation, especially when you have a great deal of information to communicate as often is the case with a building program.

It's important not to rely exclusively on the annual campaign for stewardship education in your church. The annual campaign should be only one part of a broader approach to stewardship education. It's also important to vary the approach to the annual campaign from year-to-year. Many congregations find it helpful to adopt a three or four year cycle, intentionally changing the basic strategy each year.

And remember that **prayer** is absolutely basic to the Christian life. All the effective stewardship campaign approaches we've studied include a major emphasis on prayer.

A Congregational Devotional Booklet

Many congregations have developed their own devotional booklets for the Advent (Christmas) or Lenten (Easter) seasons. Members are invited to write their own short meditations and prayers appropriate to the season and perhaps to a particular emphasis incorporated in the booklet. These are generally modeled on the pattern of devotions in *The Upper Room* or *Our Daily Bread*.

During the Spirituality and Giving Project, we encouraged congregations to develop their own devotional booklets for use during the annual stewardship campaign or during another time of the year. We were very impressed by the quality of the devotions written and also pleased by the very high percentage of readership in the congregations which used this approach.

This can be an excellent way to deepen the spiritual life and can also be a valuable addition to any campaign strategy. The process of thinking through what they want to say about stewardship strengthens the faith of those who contribute to the booklet, and the resulting devotions are of far more interest to the congregation than those from commercial sources. Sample instructions follow:

Devotional Booklet Instructions

The devotional that you write should be an expression of your own feelings or experiences about stewardship (of money, time, or talents), the importance the church or a church organization (such as a camp or college) has had in your life, or around the theme *The Desires of Your Heart*. We would like for each devotional to have a title, a recommended Bible reading, the devotion itself, and a closing prayer. Here are a number of general topics which may help you decide on your own specific topic:

- How I have felt personally blessed because of my giving to God's work through the church.
- The link I feel between financial giving and the spiritual life.
- Why I think it's important to be concerned about stewardship of the natural world – not just our financial resources.
- How I feel about the work done by a camp, college, retirement home, or other church institution.
- How I feel about the Sunday school program at our church (or about women's fellowship, etc.)
- Why I pray for the financial well-being of our church.
- How another person witnessed to me in a way that caused me to increase my level of giving.

You may decide on a topic different than those above; those are simply suggested starting points. You may prefer to write a poem or a prayer. Your devotional will be typeset to fit on a 5 1/2" x 8 1/2" page. Please try not to go over 300 words in length; there's no problem in being shorter than that. Please send or bring your completed devotional to the church office.

---

2. Begin practicing stewardship education as a twelve month process which involves children, youth, and adults.

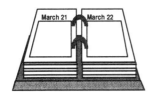

"The theory of doing stewardship education on a year-round basis is a great one," Teresa said to Jim and Frank at another breakfast meeting. "The problem is that we have too much else happening in the church. It isn't realistic to talk about money at times other than the annual campaign."

"That's exactly what we experience in our church," said Jim. "On the other hand, it make sense to me that people would be more open to hearing about stewardship concerns when we weren't actually asking them for money. They'd be a lot less defensive then."

"Some of this depends on how you define stewardship education," Frank offered. "You can do a stewardship sermon that's totally focused on giving or on the concept of stewardship, but you can also talk about stewardship and giving matters as parts of several different messages. The parables of the Good Samaritan, the Lost Coin, and the Prodigal Son all have stewardship lessons. You can share those as part of a sermon dealing with the biblical passage. And of course stewardship education isn't just what happens in worship. It needs to include Christian education, youth work, newsletter articles, and all kinds of other things."

"What about stewardship education with children?" Jim asked. "Does your church really take that seriously? In my church, we don't even want to buy offering envelopes for the kids because the Finance Committee thinks it's a waste of money."

"In my opinion, that's pretty short-sided," said Frank. "A child who receives five dollars a week of allowance can give ten percent of that to the church a lot easier than an adult who receives a thousand dollars a week. If you start doing that when you're a child, though, you can maintain the habit for a lifetime."

"What I really need to do in my church," said Teresa, "is help the Finance Committee develop a plan for stewardship education. The fact that we don't have an overall plan is why we don't do anything until we get in a panic about the annual financial campaign."

Stewardship Education

Many of us have shared in discussions about the importance of doing stewardship education on a year-round basis, but few of us have been successful in moving from discussion to implementation. The reality is that the major stewardship education push for most congregations comes in conjunction with the annual financial campaign. Certainly stewardship education should be part of the annual campaign, but that simply isn't enough. In order to deepen the spiritual basis for giving, people need considerable help understanding the relationship between their faith and their stewardship of the resources God has provided.

In the Christian Community study, we found that only 12.4% of the congregations had a systematic stewardship education program which involved every adult class on an annual basis. The percentages for youth and children were even lower. Yet the vast majority of the congregational leaders we surveyed felt that members were capable of giving significantly more than they currently are. In the congregations which surveyed the entire membership, over 78% of the members completing the surveys said that they would benefit from more opportunity to understand and discuss the significance of money in their lives and in society. We need to expand the opportunities for people to connect their giving to the spiritual life.

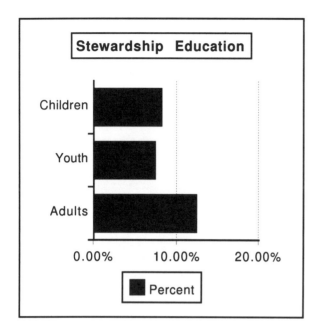

Stewardship Education

Children
Youth
Adults

0.00%   10.00%   20.00%

■ Percent

Our efforts at stewardship education emphasize stewardship of the natural world (water, air, plants, animals, ...) as well as money. **56.5%** agreed

Churches which did practice systematic stewardship education were over twice as likely to have experienced large increases in giving. Congregations not providing children with the education and practice are missing a valuable opportunity for the future – and the present. **Young adults who started systematic giving as children are seven times as likely to be tithers than those who did not.**

The churches doing year-round stewardship education indicated in phone interviews that they find people more open to talking about stewardship issues at times when a financial campaign is not in progress. They also indicated, however, that each time the church is seeking money for a particular cause opportunities for stewardship education are stimulated.

Stewardship as a Broad Concern

We found that congregations take seriously the concept that stewardship involves more than the management of our financial resources. Consider these items and the responses from church leaders:

Our efforts at stewardship education emphasize stewardship of time and talents as well as money. **91.9%** agreed

In phone interviews, we were told by many people that the traditional pledge cards they use include places for people to commit their time, talents, and prayers to God at the same time that they commit their financial resources. Church leaders were divided, however, about whether or not it was useful to have the commitment of those assets at the same time as financial giving commitments. Some felt the other commitments ceased to have meaning because it was so obvious that finances were the main target of the campaign. Others felt that the process of pledging time, talent, and prayer, as well as financial resources, was a good way to encourage a broader view of stewardship.

Financial commitment time is obviously only one occasion when a broader view of stewardship can be taught. Several of those we interviewed said that in the process of teaching stewardship, it was considerably easier to get people to talk about the stewardship of time and talent than about the stewardship of money.

Even though the percentage of those including a natural world emphasis in their stewardship education is lower than for those emphasizing time and talent, it is still true for over half the respondents. Some shared comments with us like these:

- "We'd rather talk about stewardship of the water and of farm land than about stewardship of our wealth. Most of us don't control any vast quantities of water or farm land, so those stewardship issues don't affect us so strongly."

- "I think we haven't done nearly enough to help people think about what it means to live as a fully committed steward. When we neglect to help people see that the quality of our water, the quality of our air, and the care of animal and planet life are matters of Christian stewardship, we're neglecting part of our responsibility to God."

A comprehensive stewardship education program needs to include new members. People are more receptive to considering their stewardship at the time they actually join a congregation than on any other occasion. Churches which are sensitive to those who are described as "seekers" recognize that emphasizing finances when people first come as visitors can be counter-productive. People who are afraid the church is primarily after their money will have that reinforced if they feel pressured to give during the courtship time with the church. Once they have decided to join the congregation, however, it is appropriate to talk about money with them; and they are generally open to that discussion.

A church should have a healthy respect for the reality that people donate to support needs outside of the congregation. Much has been said statistically about the higher percentages of giving which characterize churches described as fundamentalist or evangelical in contrast to the mainline Protestant denominations. While those realities are generally true, also keep in mind the fact that people in mainline Protestant churches are more likely to support a variety of needs within the community. Most of these persons are donating a greater percentage of their money than is reflected in their giving to the church. A holistic view of the gospel recognizes the importance of supporting worthy efforts which take place outside of the formal Christian community.

Stewardship education at its best needs to help people understand several basic concepts:

- That giving is part of developing a close relationship with Christ and is fundamental to the spiritual life. Ignoring stewardship when talking about church membership and about commitment to Christ is ignoring a central part of faith development.

- That giving should be on the basis of a percent of one's income rather than a specific dollar figure. In many traditions, the tithe should be the goal toward which individuals and households work. For those who have been especially blessed, however, a tithe may not represent an adequate level of giving.

- That giving to the church and to other charitable causes should be the first distribution from one's income rather than what one gives after other bills have been paid and other needs have been met.

- That parents need to help children develop regular patterns of giving.

- That a full understanding of stewardship includes time, talents, and the world in which we live as well as financial resources.

- That stewardship means being concerned not only about the ten percent or so given to the church but also about the way in which the other ninety percent of one's financial resources are used.

- That a true biblical understanding of stewardship, in which we see ourselves as caretakers rather than as owners, should include a deeper sense of concern for and obligation to the poor of the world.

- That a lifestyle based on a biblical understanding of stewardship is a goal toward which one should strive but not a goal which is quickly reached. Forgiveness and grace need to be included in our interpretation of stewardship, so that we do not end up promoting a kind of works righteousness (or financial righteousness!). We need to recognize that people are at different points in the spiritual life. Consequently, we need to utilize a broad approach to stewardship education which will help people at various stages.

Multiple Sources of Income

As suggested earlier in this chapter, each time the church seeks and receives money or other material gifts provides an opportunity for education about stewardship and giving. In thinking about church finances as a whole, it's important to remember that most churches have several potential sources of income, including:

1. The annual campaign that meets the budget or is the basis on which the budget is developed.

2. Planned special offerings during the year.

3. Spontaneous opportunities to give in response to an emerging need – especially when that need involves people who can be identified.

4. Short-term projects which invite giving over a two- to four-year period of time. Designated fund giving for things like a new ministry emphasis, a church renovation program, or a new staff member can fall into this category.

5. Fund-raising projects such as dinners and sales that provide opportunity for those not yet ready to pledge generously to become involved in support of the church.

6. Planned giving opportunities which encourage giving through wills, living trusts, life insurance policies, and other means. These are sometimes connected to an endowment fund which has been established by the church.

7. User fees from groups using church facilities and rental income from church property. Almost thirty percent of the churches we surveyed said that rental income has become an important component of their budgets. Those fees most frequently came from nursery and day care programs which utilized church facilities, but there were other nonprofit rentals as well. Fees from weddings and receptions constitute an important source of income for some churches.

8. User fees from participants in activities like music groups, study groups, Vacation Bible School, exercise groups, sports groups, and so forth. Some churches are not comfortable charging fees for any activities, but others have found this a good way to expand programming by letting those who want to participate meet the expense. If you do move in this direction, be sure to make provision for some scholarships and waivers so that persons are not excluded because of financial restrictions. It also needs to be said that people who need a scholarship or waiver are not always comfortable requesting or accepting one.

9. Sale of stocks, bonds, houses, land, vehicles, and other donated items.

10. Grants which may come from denominational sources or even from public or private foundations. A congregation starting a new outreach to "at-risk" youth, for example, can sometimes qualify for significant financial assistance from such sources.

11. Interest and investment income may be received by churches, depending on the assets being held by the church.

12. Memorial gifts in honor of persons who have been active in the life of the church.

13. Loans to help a church with a particular project. These may come from a financial services institution, from a denominational agency, or from members of the church.

14. Advanced payments on pledges when a giver benefits from paying the year before. While the church may wish to hold the money until the year for which it was intended to give support, the interest on that money may be made immediately available.

We also found an interesting variation on fees for the use of church facilities for weddings by nonmembers. Some churches have elected, instead of charging a rental fee and other wedding fees to nonmembers, to require that couples attend a certain number of worship services and church activities before the wedding date. This exposes them to the life of the church and gives people in the church opportunity to reach out to them. This approach has interesting possibilities in terms of ministry, church growth, and stewardship. Certainly a couple who joins the church will in time donate more than would have been received in rental fees. Of course, some denominational traditions restrict the use of the church for weddings to those who are members. Other churches may wish to rethink their policies in this regard.

Getting Stewardship Education Done!

In terms of structure, it is often unrealistic to expect that the existing finance or stewardship commission will be able to handle all the responsibilities of financial management, conduct the major financial campaign, and still do stewardship education. Lyle Schaller stated in *44 Ways to Expand the Financial Base of Your Congregation*: "The vast majority of Protestant congregations on this continent project unrealistic and contradictory expectations of their finance committee" (p. 145).

In the face of those expectations, expense reduction often becomes the priority. Schaller suggests that the existing finance committee be replaced with three different groups: one for stewardship education, one to develop the budget, and one to monitor expenditures. If your congregation only has fifty members, then three different committees may not be realistic, but the functions can still be assigned to different persons. If your congregation has five hundred members or five thousand members, then you need to seriously consider the use of multiple groups or committees if you are not already doing so.

A comprehensive, twelve month stewardship education program needs to consider a wide range of possible settings and strategies. Here's the plan of one congregation:

Sermons

- January: a sermon dealing with the stewardship of the natural world and containing a reminder that all of our assets in fact belong to God.

- March: a communion sermon talking about the bread and the cup as symbols, among other things, of the necessities of life which are provided to us by God and a reminder that all things come from God and belong to God.

- May: a special service near Memorial Day which includes a celebration of the lives of all those who have died in the past year and the dedication of memorial gifts which have been received. The sermon includes an emphasis on the heritage which we leave behind, including our financial assets.

- July: a sermon on the Good Samaritan which talks about the importance of sharing our assets with those in need and which lifts up some of the ways that happens through denominational agencies and through local church efforts.

- September: a drama presented by the youth instead of a sermon. The drama deals with what it means to live in the knowledge that all one has and all one is comes from the grace of God.

- October: a sermon about giving based on 2 Corinthians 9:6-12. *And God is able to provide you with every blessing in abundance, so that by always having enough of everything, you may share abundantly in every good work* [v.8]. The sermon comes the week before Celebration Sunday when pledges are dedicated on the altar. The service on Celebration Sunday emphasizes a spirit of thanksgiving for all we have received.

- November: a sermon talking about what it means to live with a total spirit of thanksgiving for what God has given to us.

- December: a sermon about the birth in the manger and the identity which Christians have with the poor of the world and with those who live in difficult circumstances. We need to reach out to those persons with financial gifts and in other ways.

Other Worship Strategies

- Offertory sentences and prayers appropriate for each week which contribute to a deeper understanding of the spiritual side of giving.

- "Minute Speakers" coinciding with each special offering taken during the year. These persons will help make connections between giving and the spiritual life in their presentations.

- A series of three "Minute Speakers" leading up to Celebration Sunday, with each one talking about his or her motivation for giving to the church.

Christian Education Classes

- Spring study of Gene Roop's book *Let the Rivers Run* by all adult classes.

- A unit on stewardship in the spring in classes for youth and children.

- A summer emphasis in Sunday school on raising money for a mission site and on understanding the needs related to that mission site. A youth trip to the mission site.

- A teacher training event at the start of the fall to help teachers of all ages be alert for opportunities to talk about stewardship with classes and groups as those opportunities naturally present themselves.

- Fall study of the Christian Community booklet *The Desires of Your Heart* (a shorter publication than this report, designed for use by individuals, classes,

and groups) by youth and adults.

- Youth group development of a video on our church's vision and outreach. The video will be shown in all of our Christian education classes and groups.

- Plans for each children's and youth class to talk about tithing and to see that all children and youth receive boxes of envelopes which they can use for their offerings.

Other Communications and Strategies

- Updates on church finances and special needs enclosed with each statement given to congregation members and other supporters.

- A schedule of articles in the church newsletter. These should include statistical information about giving patterns in the congregation.

- A series of letters of information and encouragement leading up to Celebration Sunday.

- Door-to-door visits of inactive members to encourage them to attend the special congregational dinner held on Celebration Sunday.

- Discussion by the board of the principles and goals which should undergird the process of building a budget once pledges have been received.

- A comprehensive system of letters of thanks when pledges are made to the financial campaign and when special gifts are made to various causes during the year.

- The provision of a seminar on estate planning which includes information about our endowment fund.

- The availability of an attorney to help church members who wish to remember the church in their wills or in their living trusts.

The attorney agrees to donate a certain number of hours each year, and the church will pay for any needed hours over that amount.

- A comprehensive effort after the annual meeting of the denomination to help church members understand the many needs which are being met by denominational programs. A team of three people develops and implements this plan.

- A tax planning letter to members during the last quarter of the year. This letter includes the suggestion of giving stocks or other appreciated assets as an alternative to cash because of the tax savings which may be possible.

- The assignment of each special offering to a specific group or to a team of people for the development of a comprehensive promotional plan including not only the minute speaker but also newsletter articles, posters, and sometimes the involvement or a class or group.

- A system of regular review of giving patterns by the treasurer and the financial secretary. When persons who have been regular contributors stop doing so, a pastoral or deacon contact is arranged. The change in regular giving may indicate a personal problem or the presence of a negative attitude toward something which has happened in the life of the church. Whatever the reason, it's important for the church not to ignore what has happened.

- Three special fund-raising efforts during the year for special needs to give people opportunity to help the church in that way:

  - A dinner to raise money for a local homeless shelter.

  - A garage sale to raise money for renovation of Sunday school rooms.

  - A church-wide bazaar to raise

money for overseas missions.

A special effort is made to involve persons in these activities who are not among the higher givers in the church. This provides a good way for them to help and also for them to learn more about the difference made by the generosity of people.

Our Wealth and the Needs of the World

Many of us need a healthier perspective on the wealth that we have relative to the needs of the world. In "Deciding to Make a Difference," John and Sylvia Ronsvalle point out that: "Since about 1950, a new situation has existed in the U.S. Instead of the majority of people being poor, the majority of people had more than needed for basic needs and still had money to spend. In 1993, per capita income in the U.S. was over 200% greater, after taxes and after inflation, than in 1933, the depth of the Great Depression" (*The Abingdon Guide to Funding Ministry*, p. 106).

That wealth gives us great potential to make a difference in the lives of others. Studies of the giving of church members confirm that most of us are donating between 2% and 3% of our incomes to charitable causes. If that figure were to rise to 10% from all Christians, the amount of money available for mission outreach – spreading the gospel, fighting hunger, helping children and youth, caring for the elderly, working for peace – would be staggering. Those needs exist around the world.

While rapid electronic communication keeps us well informed about many events around the world, we do not always connect personally with those who are in need. The Spirituality and Giving Project made us very aware that a majority of local congregations are not enthusiastic about giving money to distant mission work – in large measure because they do not understand the level of need which exists in other countries.

It's important for people to understand the needs which exist within our congregations and our communities. It's also important for them to understand the needs which exist around the world. Our efforts at stewardship education should help people understand the potential for tremendous impact on those needs which every congregation has. Youth mission trips and other efforts which give people first-hand exposure to such needs can make a difference.

3. Encourage tithing or proportionate giving.

"The secret to developing giving in your congregation is to push tithing," Brad said to Mary, who pastored the church across the street from his. "I've not done any other single thing which has made so much difference in giving in my church."

"That's okay for you Methodists," she responded, "but it's not so easy for Disciples of Christ. We're historically opposed to legalism of any kind, and tithing smacks of legalism."

"Of course it does. That's why it works!" laughed Brad. "We may believe in salvation by faith and not works, but we've all got a little works righteousness in us. I admit that the Bible doesn't say as much about tithing as some people claim, but it's a standard people can understand. It has a significant place in the history of Christianity, and most people know what it means."

"I'll agree that there's a place for proportionate giving. The more you have, the more God expects from you. We need to get that concept across. The problem for me, personally rather than as a Disciple of Christ pastor, is that tithing seems a little too much to ask of someone who is trying to get by on social security and a small pension, and it doesn't seem to me nearly enough for a physician or executive who's earning three hundred thousand a year. I don't want to push people too hard on the lower end, and I don't want to limit giving on the higher end."

"Well, unless Disciples are a lot different than Methodists in their giving patterns, you don't have to be worried about limiting on the higher end. My experience is that the people who have lower incomes are more likely to tithe than the people with higher incomes. Ironically some of the people with fixed incomes in my church are the most consistent tithers. What the tithe does is give a target, something to aim for. I agree that we shouldn't make people feel pressured and that we shouldn't say that tithing is an adequate standard for everyone."

"With the average person giving maybe two or three percent of his or her income to the church and other charities, it certainly would be wonderful if the whole congregation would tithe," Mary agreed. "We'd have more money than we knew what to do with if everyone tithed. At least we could be encouraging proportionate giving, even in a Disciples congregation."

"Pushing tithing has worked for us," Brad affirmed again. "We certainly don't have everyone in the congregation tithing, but we've gone from only three households in the church tithing to fifty households tithing in the last three years, and giving is up significantly for everyone. We've encouraged people to work toward a tithe, and I think the strategy is continuing to work."

The Tithe

The practice of tithing goes back to our Old Testament roots, and for many the tithe has been the time-honored standard for giving. Some, like Mary, make the case that there are persons who cannot, without harm to themselves or their families, afford to give a full 10% tithe. A strong argument can also be made that persons with exceptional resources should give more than 10%.

The approach is biblical, traditional, and effective. It's also an approach most easily developed as a child and a teenager. Churches which are truly looking toward the future help their children and young people begin developing the habit. Some helpful biblical references on tithing:

- Genesis 28:10-22
- Numbers 18:25-27
- Deuteronomy 14:22-29, 26:11-13
- Malachi 3, 6, 12
- Luke 11:42
- Hebrews 7:1-10

In preaching and teaching about tithing, be sure to emphasize that the Bible conveys the importance of setting aside the money for God FIRST rather than of giving from leftovers.

For those churches not comfortable with the concept of tithing, focus attention instead on the biblical case for proportionate giving, which is very strong, and may sound better to some persons than the flat 10%. Deuteronomy 16:17, for example, says:

All shall give as they are able, according to the blessing of the LORD your God that he has given you.

Proverbs 3:9-10 says:

Honor the LORD with your substance and with the first fruits of all your produce; then your barns will be filled with plenty, and your vats will be bursting with wine.

Another important passage comes in the story of the widow's offering in Mark 12:41-44, in which Jesus says:

For all of them have contributed out of their abundance; but she out of her poverty has put in everything she had, all she had to live on [v.44].

The tithe was not the standard for her – she gave all that she had.

In our study, we found that 42% of the congregational leaders responding felt that their church encouraged tithing. In response to follow-up questions, however, most acknowledged not encouraging tithing in very specific ways. Those which were using specific strategies to increase the number of persons tithing were showing impressive results. Those churches showing the best results from an emphasis on tithing or proportionate giving were characterized by:

- An overall strategy which talks about the importance of tithing or proportionate giving. That means more than a passing reference in a sermon or one line in the annual giving materials.

- References to tithing in all campaign materials.

- Clear references to tithing made by the pastor and also by some lay persons (as minute speakers or in articles or group settings).

- The provision of a chart or of stages for increased giving which clearly show tithing as the goal for which one should strive.

- The encouragement of tithing in children's classes and youth groups.

- In many instances, an annual breakfast or other support group strategy for those who are tithing.

The First Ten Group

Some churches which choose to promote tithing in a major way form a special club or a group of those who are tithing to provide mutual support and added incentive to others. It helps to know that other people are giving at the same percentage level, and people may decide that they would like to be part of such a group. Several such groups have been formed by pastors who have said to their congregations (something like this):

My family and I take seriously the need to generously respond to God for all that we have received. For us, this means giving at least ten percent or our income, or a tithe, to the church. I would like to invite those who are interested in giving at a higher level to meet with us for breakfast this coming Saturday at eight o'clock at the church. We'll talk together about the benefits of tithing, and we'll covenant to pray for each other in our efforts at giving generously to the church.

Such an event can become known as the Tithing Breakfast and can become an annual ritual. Others may form a Tithers Club or a Ten Percent Club or a First Ten Group (setting aside the first ten percent for God).

There are traditions in which having an organization of those who are setting a higher standard of giving could be viewed as boastful or as lacking in humility. If you are part of such a tradition, then you need to respect that danger. You may find it better not to give a particular name or identity to the group but simply invite people who want to tithe to come together on an annual basis for mutual support and prayer.

Obviously it's a mistake to give any decision-making power or authority to a group composed of people based only on their level of giving to the church. While those persons who tithe are likely to be among your most deeply committed and thus are likely to be in a variety of leadership positions, you don't want financial giving along to be the criterion for leadership.

Being part of a group of others who tithe, even if meeting only once a year, can provide good mutual support and encouragement. The initiation of such a group can be a way of moving several households at once to the level of the tithe. You can also emphasize tithing without the use of any group.

Getting to the Tithe

Many of us who are highly committed to the life of the church increase our giving on a percentage basis from year-to-year. For example, some people have become tithers by increasing the amount of giving to the church by one percent a year – giving 4% the first year, 5% the second year, 6% the third year, and continuing until the 10% level has been reached. The next page shows a ladder approach to increased proportionate giving, and you may well decide that you want to utilize the diagram and chart in your giving campaign or in stewardship education during the year.

(Variations on ladders and stairways appear in so many materials that it is impossible to know who originally conceived the idea. It is broadly used and generally effective.)

Those of us involved in campaign leadership, however, need to stay aware that large numbers of people make big leaps in giving rather than smaller systematic increases. The person who is currently giving $300 a year to the budget of the church from an income of $45,000 a year is not likely to gradually move to the level of a tithe. That person is more likely, for example, to make a move from $300 a year to $2,000 a year; stay flat on giving for two or three more years; and then be moved to go directly to a tithe. It's important not to focus so hard on a one-step-at-a-time view of increased giving that people are actually talked out of larger increases!

The practice of tithing can most easily be developed with children and youth. Include pledge cards or intention of giving cards for them in any campaign you do.

The Abundant Life

In his thought-provoking book *Living Faith*, Jimmy Carter writes about some of the ways in which we deprive ourselves of the abundant life which God wishes to give us. Speaking of people his own age, he wrote:

We learned to live cautiously, to fear debt, and to limit our ambitions and the chances we were willing to take. Most of us still want to be sure we don't give away too much, so we always parcel out a little at a time, making sure we hold back more than we might need.

As a consequence, we often underestimate the gifts we have from God: life, talent, ability, knowledge, freedom, influence, and plenty of opportunities to do something extraordinary. We have to remember that our lives will become shrunken if we act only from a cautious sense of duty. [p. 237]

Tithing should not be permitted to become simply a sense of duty or obligation. Our approach to interpreting tithing or proportionate giving needs to emphasize the abundant, joyful life to which Christ calls us. Tithing is a way to stop holding so much back – to move forward in our relationships with God. And tithing should never be presented as the limit on what we give or do.

"All shall give as they are able, according to the blessing of the LORD your God that he has given you."   **Deuteronomy 16:17**

"Take delight in the LORD, and he will give you the desires of your heart."   **Psalm 37:4**

Over 10%
10% - A Tithe
9%
8%
7%
6%
5%
4%
3%
2%
1%

Raising Your Level of Giving –
One Step at a Time

Find your place on the ladder. Can you move your percentage of giving up one step this year? Then up another step the next year? Keep moving a step at a time until you've reached at least the level of a tithe (10%).

Or for a different perspective, compare your level of giving with your income using this chart. Can you increase your giving by a step, moving toward a tithe?

Growth in Giving as % of Annual Income

Income	3%	4%	5%	6%	7%	8%	9%	10%
100,000	3000	4000	5000	6000	7000	8000	9000	10000
75,000	2250	3000	3750	4500	5250	6000	6750	7500
65,000	1950	2600	3250	3900	4550	5200	5850	6500
55,000	1650	2200	2750	3300	3850	4400	4950	5500
45,000	1350	1800	2250	2700	3150	3600	4050	4500
35,000	1050	1400	1750	2100	2450	2800	3150	3500
25,000	750	1000	1250	1500	1750	2000	2250	2500
15,000	450	600	750	900	1050	1200	1350	1500
10,000	300	400	500	600	700	800	900	1000

4. Let people make pledges and regular gifts to more than a single fund, encouraging rather than discouraging designated giving.

"Does your church have a unified budget?" Teresa asked Frank in a telephone conversation.

"You mean, do we have all our expenses integrated into a single budget against which people make pledges?"

"Yes."

"We like to think that we do, but we don't," Frank answered. "I don't think any church really does. There are always going to be some special funds and special gifts. Why are you interested in knowing?"

"The board at my church is really adamant about not having more than two special offerings a year. They want to integrate all the needs into the single budget and push people for the maximum possible pledge to that budget. They think that having too many special offerings or other funds will keep people from giving the support they should to the unified budget. I think we're missing out on some income by not giving people opportunity to give extra support to things they want to see happen."

"Doesn't your church accept memorial gifts for designated purposes?"

"We have new carpeting in the sanctuary in memory of the life of Hattie Bainbridge," Teresa said.

"Exactly. And I'll bet you have a youth group, a women's group, or a men's group with its own budget and its own projects that aren't supported by the church budget."

"Sure. We have all three. And people do fund-raising projects and collect donations for those groups."

"What about Sunday school class funds?" Frank asked.

"We have two adult classes with their own bank accounts. One of them donates very heavily to the Heifer Project. They probably give three or four thousand dollars a year. The other class is our oldest, and they use money to provide flowers and gifts for people who are confined to the hospital, a nursing home, or their own homes."

"I think every church has some funds like those. It's almost impossible to have a truly unified budget."

"But if you have too many separate funds, can't that start to hurt the basic budget of the church?"

"I suppose there may be a point at which it would, but usually you aren't asking people to pledge to those funds. You simply accept donations, and groups like the ones you mentioned often do fund-raising projects."

"Of course you accept pledges to a building fund or a capital campaign fund if you build a new church or do a major expansion," Teresa said.

"Right. And two years ago, we tried something different when we wanted to expand our youth ministry. In addition to the General Budget and the Building Fund, we decided to give people opportunity to pledge to a Youth Outreach Fund. We wanted to take our youth pastor from part-time to full-time, and we wanted to hire another part-time person to help. We promoted pledges and gifts to that fund as well as to the General Budget and the Building Fund. What happened is that some of our people who wanted to see the youth program improved, especially parents, dug deeper and gave very generously to the Youth Outreach Fund. We actually exceeded our goal."

"What did you do with the extra money?"

"We used it for renovation of the youth rooms. That was consistent with the purpose for which it was given."

"Was your General Fund hurt by people pledging to the Youth Outreach Fund?"

"No. The General Fund did just fine," Frank responded. "We only had one person who apparently cut his giving to the General Fund in order to give more to the Youth Outreach Fund. Most of the people made increases in giving to the General Fund and gave extra to the Youth Outreach Fund. What made it exciting is that we had perhaps a dozen families who hadn't been giving much to the church at all who made really significant pledges to the Youth Outreach Fund. They've started a different pattern of giving, and that will help us not only now but in the years ahead."

"But you didn't know for sure that letting people pledge to the Youth Outreach Fund wouldn't hurt your General Fund giving."

"That's right. We didn't. We worked with a fund-raising consultant, and he suggested we include a line on the pledge forms which gave the Finance Committee permission to move money between funds if necessary for the overall welfare of the church. People could strike out that permission-giving line if they wanted, but everyone was comfortable with it. If we'd ended up with a lot of money in the Youth Outreach Fund at the expense of the General Fund or the Building Fund, we'd have made some adjustments and reported those to the congregation. That didn't happen."

"A lot of the younger people in my church," Teresa observed, "have a strong need to feel that their giving is making a difference – making something happen. Giving to the unified budget doesn't help them get that feeling of satisfaction. The older people in our church feel that isn't a very mature way of

giving, but I'm young enough myself to understand it. Supporting a Youth Outreach Fund like you let people do in your church would be a lot more exciting than just giving to the General Fund."

"It's one of the ways to help people move forward in their giving," Frank agreed. "If you don't give people opportunities like that, you simply are going to lose some of the generosity of which people are capable."

How Many Funds?

The concept of the unified budget has won broad acceptance in Protestant and Anabaptist congregations, and most churches need to have the majority of the core ministries included in a single budget. Relying exclusively on the unified budget, however, increasingly means missing out on the extra giving which some persons can be motivated to provide in support of more specific causes or needs. Besides that, as Frank pointed out, almost none of our churches have budgets that are truly unified.

Leaders who work in stewardship find two contrasting kinds of systems:

- **The donor-based system** in which donors make the decisions about where their money goes based on their understanding of the needs of others and on their own interests and sense of compassion.

- **The unified-budget system**, which has the financial decisions of the church made by a group of persons who study the needs inside and outside of the congregation with great care and then develop a unified budget to which people make their contributions. Some prefer calling the unified-budget system a mission-based system.

Traditional church fund-raising often carries with it the assumption that a group of people who study the multitude of needs which exist can make more informed decisions than individuals acting on their own. There is considerable wisdom in that view. Yet that doesn't change the reality that increasing numbers of persons want to have more direct involvement in determining what happens with their money.

One of the reasons that United Way organizations are having difficulty in many communities isn't because those United Ways have done something "wrong." It's because people are wanting more involvement in determining what is done with their gifts and often want to support causes that are more experimental than those which traditional United Way organizations have funded. Many United Ways are in the process of changing how they select projects and are soliciting considerably more input from supporters and from community organizations.

People of the so-called boomer generation and today's young adults are not as likely as older adults to give generously to a single, unified budget. They are more likely to give generously when they feel that their giving is clearly making a difference and can see what happens as a result of their gifts. Some of this desire is met through special offerings, but that same desire can result in very significant increases in giving when they have opportunity to pledge and give to a specific cause over the course of one or more years. Consider some examples:

- New church construction.
- Major church renovation.
- The addition of an employed youth worker.
- The support of a missionary.
- The establishment of a center for the homeless.
- The creation of a youth center.
- Improvements to make the church fully accessible to persons with disabilities.
- A major evangelism emphasis.
- The sponsorship of a seminary student.

In some instances the additional fund can provide a means of voting for a new program. If sufficient people are willing to support the program, it proceeds. It's not unusual to find some persons who will give over a thousand dollars above their regular pledge to a specific fund in order to make a ministry happen.

In offering a designated giving option, the church can provide a short statement on the intention of giving card which says: "In the event that the Finance Committee finds itself short of needed funds for core ministries of our church, I give permission for the designation of my pledge to be changed." That provides the opportunity for designated giving but also protects the core ministries. Persons who are not comfortable giving that authority to the Finance Committee (or another appropriate group) can strike those words from the pledge form. Church leaders, of course, want to do everything possible to honor the designations persons have made.

Currently about 26% of the mainline congregations we surveyed are actively encouraging some form of designated giving, and the results have been positive in almost every instance – often at very significant levels. Almost 31% of the congregations we surveyed, however, indicate that they discourage designated giving. The majority of those congregations are not showing the increases in overall giving that is reflected by the 26% that encourage at least some amount of designated giving.

Note that designated giving for particular causes can have spectacular results. A Miracle Sunday offering for a major mission project [new nursery school, new staff member, building renovation, . . .] can raise between one-fourth and three times a year's budget. A three-year capital funds drive can generate two-and-a-half times a single year's budget. [Slightly over 9% of the churches we surveyed have tried a Miracle Sunday appeal.]

Second-mile giving or special fund appeals for projects such as a staff addition can be effective strategies. When people are pleased with the result, they will generally continue to support the position.

A typical multiple-fund pledging opportunity would permit people to give money to:

- Regular operating expenses

- Payments on a church debt, for a new building project, or on the creation of a new staff position or outreach effort

- Missions

Note the sample pledge cards/forms which follow this page.

Memorial Gifts

Memorial gifts can be an especially good means of encouraging designated giving to specific projects. Most churches receive substantial amounts in memorial gifts each year as people want to honor the memory of a friend or family member who has died. Increasing numbers of churches are developing "wish lists" of needs which cannot be met from the regular budget but might be fulfilled by designated gifts such as memorial funds. Attractive brochures incorporating those needs and the cost of each need are broadly distributed in the congregation so that members are aware of the opportunity for giving. If your church does not have a policy concerning memorial gifts, one should be considered. An example of a congregational memorial gifts policy and a sample project list follow the sample pledge cards/forms.

Commitment Form

Because of Christ's great love and the abundant gifts I've/we've received, I/we intend to support the ministries of our church by giving the following:

$_____   _per week
                     _per month
                     _per year

Name(s): _____

Address: _____

The Desires of

Your Heart

Trust in the Lord, and do good. . . .
Take delight in the Lord, and
He will give you
The desires of your heart.
Psalm 37:3-4

Commitment Form

Because of Christ's great love and the abundant gifts I've/we've received, I/we intend to support the ministries of our church by giving the following:

$_____   to the general budget
                    _per week   _per month   _per year

$_____   to the building fund
                    _per week   _per month   _per year

$_____   to the children's ministry fund
                    _per week   _per month   _per year

In the event of a crisis in church finances, I/we give permission for money donated by me/us to be transferred among those funds for the good of the congregation. I/We understand that our own intention of giving can be changed at any time by notifying the church office.

The Desires of

Your Heart

Trust in the Lord, and do good. . . .
Take delight in the Lord, and
He will give you
The desires of your heart.
Psalm 37:3-4

Name(s): _____

Address: _____

These are sample pledge/intention of giving forms. There are many other possibilities, limited only by the creativity of your group. See the form on the next page which also provides for multiple funds but does not specify the options in addition to the general budget.

Commitment Form

Because of Christ's great love and the abundant gifts I've/we've received, I/we intend to support the ministries of our church by giving the following:

$_____   to the general budget
                __per week   __per month __per year

$_____   to _____
                __per week   __per month __per year

$_____   to _____
                __per week   __per month __per year

In the event of a crisis in church finances, I/we give permission for money donated by me/us to be transferred among those funds for the good of the congregation. I/We understand that our own intention of giving can be changed at any time by notifying the church office.

Name(s): _____

Address: _____

The Desires of Your Heart

Trust in the Lord, and do good. . . .
Take delight in the Lord, and
He will give you
The desires of your heart.
Psalm 37:3-4

Memorial Gifts, Bequests, and Special Gifts

Gifts in memory of loved ones, bequests from wills and grants from living trusts, and other special gifts are very important to the life of our congregation. We always intend to honor the intent of gifts which are offered, and we also want to recognize those gifts to the congregation except in those instances where anonymity is preferred. These policies and operational guidelines are designed to help all involved understand how such gifts are handled.

1. Each spring, every commission and organized group in the church gives the Stewardship Commission a list of projects with approximate dollar amounts attached which might be funded by memorial gifts, bequests, or other special gifts.

Stewardship compiles a list from all those sources, prepares a brochure, and uses broad distribution of the brochure and other publicity opportunities to generate support for those projects. If Stewardship has a concern about the wisdom of pursuing a particular project which has been suggested, Stewardship shares in conversation with the group making the suggestion and, if necessary, will ask the board to resolve the matter.

2. The Stewardship Commission names a Memorials and Special Gifts Secretary who maintains records of the projects which have been proposed, the gifts received, and other actions in this area.

When a gift has been designated for a project already on the approved list, then the Secretary will authorize the treasurer to distribute the funds for the project (or, when appropriate, to hold them until other funds have been received to meet the need for the project). The Memorials and Bequests Secretary will send notes of appreciation to those persons making such gifts or to the families of those persons (using the church office's help as appropriate).

3. When funds are received or scheduled to be received for projects which are not on the approved list, the Memorials and Bequests Secretary or another person designated by the Stewardship Commission will communicate with the appropriate persons or organizations to secure approval for the projects. If there are valid reasons for not doing a project for which funds have been given, those will be explained to the donor or to the family of the donor and alternative projects suggested. If funds are received for a project which has already been completed, alternatives will be suggested to the donor or to the donor's family. In those instances where no agreement can be reached, funds, if already received, will be returned to the donor or the donor's family with appreciation for their thoughtfulness.

4. When funds are received or scheduled to be received and have not been designated, then the Stewardship Commission will determine the projects or areas in which the funds should be spent. Input from the donor or the donor's family will be sought whenever possible and appropriate.

5. The Stewardship Commission will share reports on memorials, bequests, and other special gifts with the Board at its regular meetings. The Stewardship Commission will seek prior approval from the Board before spending undesignated gifts which are in excess of $5,000.

6. The Stewardship Commission urges people who are preparing wills and living trusts to resist the temptation to closely designate what is given. This is because the circumstances of the church and the ministry needs in the community can change between the drafting of a will or living trust and the time that the actions are carried out. Gifts given directly to our church's endowment fund or unrestricted gifts are the ones which can be worked with most creatively. If such gifts are indeed designated, then donors are encouraged to include a provision which lets the church exercise its own judgment if the designated project is no longer possible or if there are more pressing needs weighing on the leadership of the church.

7. In addition to the brochure mentioned in number one above, Stewardship will seek other means of publicizing opportunities for memorials, bequests, life insurance gifts, living trust gifts, and other special gifts.

Special Gift Projects

There are times when all of us want to do something extra for the church. Those times can include:

- The desire to give money in memory of a person who has been important in our lives.
- The receipt of an unexpected bonus at work.
- The receipt of an inheritance or proceeds from a living trust.
- The receipt of an income tax refund.
- Simply a time when we feel especially thankful to God and wish to do something in addition to our regular giving to the church.

The projects on this list have been suggested by various groups in our organizational structure. The church office can tell you about the current status of a project: whether or not it has already been funded or what funding is needed in order to complete it. Some larger projects come about because a number of different persons make gifts to that cause.

You can contribute to a specific project by placing a check in the offering plate, sending one to the church office, or bringing one to the church office. Please mark on the check or on an attached note the specific project you wish to fund or help fund. If you are making a gift in memory of a particular person, please indicate that as well. If your gift is in memory of a particular person, it isn't necessary to designate a project unless there is one you especially want to fund; often the family will make a decision about a project after all funds have been received.

Projects Under $30

Pew Bibles $15 each
300 needed
Altar Flower Arrangement $25
Church Library Books $20 each
$20 is an average; more and less expensive books are available. A committee makes the selections.
Choral Anthem $25 a set
$25 is an average; more and less expensive music is available. A committee makes the selections.

A Month of America On Line for our Children's Computer Center $20
Twelve months
Fresh Food Coupons $25
When people use our emergency food pantry, we can supply them with canned foods but they also need milk, fruit, and other fresh items. We get a bargain price on coupons from a local grocery. Your $25 gift buys $35 worth of food. We need at least two coupons a week.

Projects Between $30 and $100

Nursery School/Day Care Toys $30-50
These are durable toys which last a long time and withstand heavy use!
Padded Chairs for Fellowship Hall $50 each
200 Needed
Programs for our Children's Computer Center $30 each
$30 is an average; more and less expensive programs are available. A committee makes the selections.
A Meal for Saturday Kid's Church $50 each
Meals are served 50 weeks a year, and many of those participating are from low income families.

Projects Between $100 and $500

Classroom Television Set $250 each
2 needed
Classroom Video Player $250 each
2 needed
Classroom TV/Video Cart $150 each
2 needed
Youth Room Sofa $500
Youth Room Lounge Chairs $200 each
6 needed
Youth Room Bulletin Board $125
Youth Room Microwave $200
Youth Room Refrigerator $500
Choir Robes $125 each
40 needed
Nursery School Scholarship $450 each
Covers one semester. 10 needed a year.

Projects Over $500

Youth Room Carpeting $1,600
Youth Director's Office Carpeting $800
Improved Sanctuary Sound System $10,000
Air Conditioning Sunday School Rooms $45,000
Summer Children's Outreach Intern $6,000
Video Camera Equipment $1,500
For use in Christian Education

5. Provide opportunity for people to give from both checking and savings.

"The strategy you suggested about the Youth Outreach Fund sounded really good to me," Teresa shared with Frank. "We've been talking about a part-time Christian education director here but can never seem to find the money in the budget. Maybe the answer is that we should go outside the regular budget."

"It certainly worked for us," Frank affirmed.

"But I'll bet you didn't get as much extra giving for that as for the Building Fund."

"We didn't get as much, but we also didn't need as much. The Building Fund was for a major expansion."

"Right. But my experience is that people will always dig deeper for a building program than for anything else. You can't get them to do as much for missions or even for a special youth outreach."

"On the whole, I'd have to agree with you," Frank responded. "On the other hand, I think it's important to recognize some of the differences between a capital funds campaign for a new building or major renovation and special fund requests like missions, youth work, or Christian education directors. Most people figure they are only going to have to give to a capital funds campaign in the church a couple of times over the course of their lives. They assume the mission need, the youth need, and the Christian education need, even though they are in different funds, are going to continue to be present. For a special one-time need – or at least one time in recent years – people who have a lot of assets will dig into their savings, their accumulated wealth. That makes a huge difference in what some can afford to do."

"But they don't feel they can do that year-after-year. I see what you mean. But can't they be persuaded to go into those funds for something other than a building campaign?"

"It takes a little more work; but yes, they can be persuaded," Frank agreed. "You have to be realistic though. It depends on how much they have. Suppose a retired member has a quarter of a million dollars in mutual funds plus a small pension and social security. That quarter of a million dollars may seem like a lot of money to you and me, but think about what it really means. The person doesn't want to spend all the dividends, interest, and earnings in any given year, or the worth of the funds goes down. If all the money earned keeps getting spent year-after-year, then ten years from now that quarter of a million dollars won't have the same value it has now. You have to keep increasing the principal to keep up with inflation. Suppose the money earns 12% a year. The retired person wants to reinvest 4%, so that leaves 8% to supplement the pension and social security income."

"So the quarter of a million yields about $20,000 a year," he continued. "If the pension and social security income that person has aren't especially high, then that isn't a lot of money. If that member give you a $25,000 gift from accumulated assets, that's going to cost the member $2,000 a year of income. A person isn't going to do that more than once a decade. The appeal to the building fund is a lot more likely to net that gift than another kind of appeal."

"The example helps me," Teresa agreed. "On the other hand, I'm not saying that the person should give a tenth of his or her assets each time there's a special fund appeal. A five thousand dollar gift would have a lot less negative impact."

"That's true. And the other part is that we need to help people think about giving from their accumulated assets. From the standpoint of Christian stewardship, the accumulated assets belong to God just as much as the regular income. What's important is to have sensitivity to where people are at. We want to raise the possibility of their giving from their savings without causing them to feel pressured or to feel that we are insensitive to their need to adequately provide for the future."

How Many Pockets?

Some fund-raisers refer to what Frank and Teresa are discussing as the "two pocket" strategy. People have money in two different pockets. The first comes from what they actively earn in employment or what they receive each month from investment return, social security, or pension (money most likely to go into a checking account). The second comes from what they have saved or accumulated over the years – some of this may literally be in a savings account but much may be in mutual funds, stocks, bonds, real estate, life insurance cash value, or similar places.

For younger persons in the church, the checking account is the only source from which giving is likely to come. For older members of the congregation, however, there may be more available in accumulated assets than in current income. Increasing numbers of retired persons have the ability to give to major causes from assets without damaging their overall security. Churches undertaking a substantial building program obviously encourage people to consider asset giving, but that is not the only time that such requests are effective. If your church is making a major expansion in ministry over a three year period, it may be appropriate to encourage people to give from assets where possible. Many churches are establishing separate endowment funds for the purpose of encouraging giving from the "second pocket."

Giving from "savings" should include the option of donating substantial noncash items as well. People may benefit considerably from giving the church land, buildings, life insurance policies, stocks, bonds, and similar items. There are tax rules with which donors must comply, and the extent of the benefit derived from the gift relative to taxable income will depend on following those rules. Because those are subject to change, always recommend that people check with their accountant before making such gifts. **For most donors, the effect of the tax rules is extremely positive – letting them deduct the full value of an appreciated asset given to the church even though they may have paid far less for the item many years before.** If the donor were instead to sell the item, then there would often be taxes to pay on the increase in value of the item.

In the survey conducted as part of the Spirituality and Giving Project, we found that only 24% of the congregations did anything to encourage people to give stocks, insurance policies, property, or similar assets as well as regular cash gifts. Most churches can gain by making members more aware of the advantages of giving appreciated assets.

Your church may find it worthwhile to form a relationship with a local attorney or accountant who can give counsel to donors about noncash gifts. Publicizing the availability of that help is one way to encourage such giving.

At the time of this writing, for federal tax purposes, the donor is the one who establishes the value of the gift. The receipt from the church should describe the item received and the general condition of the item. The church may have to assign a value for reporting to the I.R.S. when the gift is a large one, but that is the only time the church should assign the value. If the church sells the item (bonds, stocks, land, etc.), then that obviously does provide a figure which may be useful to the donor. Appraisals, however, should be left to the donor. The I.R.S. generally requires a formal appraisal for an asset worth more than $5,000.

The church should have available a supply of IRS Form 8283 for "Noncash Charitable Contributions." Donors need to file that form for noncash gifts over $500. While the donor completes the form, the church having it available is another way to encourage such gifts and to make the process easier for the donor.

There is a part of Form 8283 which asks for a signature from the church acknowledging receipt of the gift. That does not mean the church is concurring with the value of the gift.

Form 8282 is one which the church must file with the I.R.S. if the church sells or disposes of the donated property within two years of the date the property was received. This is a reporting requirement on the church and is referred to on Form 8283, which is completed by the donor. A copy of the completed 8282 also goes to the donor.

Some clergy like to make a special stewardship emphasis at the end of the tax year so that they can give counsel and encouragement to those considering last minute gifts to improve their tax liability situations. A gift of appreciated stocks or bonds can be an excellent way for persons to lower current tax liability.

Many people of wealth feel that it is impossible for them to give generously because they are not "liquid." Few people keep large sums of money sitting in bank checking accounts, and savings accounts have limited use because of the relatively low interest which they pay. Money can be in stocks, bonds, land, real estate, businesses, and other investments which may not be readily available. People need encouragement to recognize that accumulated assets are still a resource for giving.

Endowment Funds

Some churches have established endowment funds as separate incorporations to which persons are encouraged to make gifts, especially those out of their assets. Endowment funds are usually set up with more restrictions on the use of the money than is the case on money given directly to the on-going funds of the church. Endowment funds normally:

- Are established to spend from the interest/dividends earned rather than from the principal. In an emergency situation for the church establishing the fund, there may be a provision for dipping into the principal, but that would require special approval – perhaps from a congregational meeting.

- Are managed for a balance between the production of income and the growth of the principal. The manage-

ment of such funds is ideally done by professionals rather than by volunteers. Some denominational agencies offer the service of managing such funds, and generally do an excellent job. Conservative church members will sometimes be more comfortable if the management is through a local financial institution. Policies vary with denominations and with financial institutions on the minimum level of funds necessary for professional management to be available.

- Audited by an outside accountant (which can, of course, be a good idea for any funds of the church).

A basic formula for the distribution of available funds each year is generally established. An example would be:

- 20% to scholarships for college, seminary, camps, and training opportunities.

- 10% to capital improvements for the church.

- 10% to the general budget of the church to be used in accordance with current priorities by the church.

- 30% to outreach to the community through specialized ministries or by donation to agencies doing work consistent with the goals of the church.

- 30% to the wider mission of the church through denominational mission programs or other opportunities.

The formula, of course, varies with the specific situation of the congregation. A church located in the same town as a church-related college might designate a significant percentage of available funds for the work of the college. An endowment fund initially established with a grant or bequest from someone deeply concerned about children and youth might include a high percentage for ministries with those age levels.

Those who are wise in establishing an endowment fund make provision for the formula of distribution to be changed if the needs of the church change. Authorization for such a change may come from a board action or from a congregational meeting, depending on the local church's organization.

Some persons have serious reservations about gifts to endowment funds. They are fearful that a large endowment fund can have a negative impact on the current giving of members of the church. They also fear that an endowment fund could keep the church going when in fact it has run its course and should not continue. There are a few examples of very small congregations with very large endowment funds, which it would appear should be supporting something other than the property and staff which are serving a shrinking body of believers.

Many churches in the United States and Canada have an older membership which is currently providing a large proportion of the overall financial support. Many of those churches will face a transition between the time of the loss of support from those older members and the time that younger members have the resources and the commitment to equal that financial support. Generous gifts from those older members through current noncash gifts (like stocks and real estate), bequests, and living trusts can provide crucial financial support for that transition time. If people have been encouraged to give 10% of their incomes in life, there is a certain logic to encouraging them to give ten percent of their assets at the end of their lives. Some, of course, can give more; but the 10% figure helps provide a guideline.

There are steps which can be taken to lessen the possibility of negative impact from endowment fund gifts. Some of those have already been discussed. Consider:

- A provision which keeps endowment funds or the earnings from those funds beyond a certain percentage from being used for any current expense except by a full congregational vote.

- A requirement that most of the funds be used for some kind of outreach.

- The strategic use of publicity to keep the congregation informed about the good being accomplished in missions and other outreach through the endowment fund.

While there certainly are valid reasons to be careful about how an endowment fund is established and the guidelines for its operation, the potential gains from having such a fund are much greater than the concerns. For every church which has experienced problems in current giving because of an endowment fund, there are many more churches which have experienced revitalization and improved outreach because of an endowment fund.

In our study, we found that about 18% of the congregations had a separate endowment fund *or* another distinct fund from the regular budget to which people were encouraged to make major gifts through wills, living trusts, or donation of current assets. Less than half of those actually had a separately incorporated endowment fund. Congregations with large numbers of older members should be giving serious consideration to the establishment of an endowment fund and to educational efforts to encourage people to consider such gifts. The launching of an endowment fund should include a clear vision of what can be accomplished with that fund; it also should be combined with educational efforts to help people understand how to give appreciated assets and how to remember the church in their wills or living trusts.

Younger members of the church can be encouraged to consider purchasing life insurance policies with the church named as a beneficiary. In some instances, there may be benefits in the church being the owner of the policy with the member paying the premium. This provides a means by which a member with very few accumulated assets can provide a potentially substantial gift to the endowment fund of the church. Talk with a good insurance agent and a tax lawyer for a fuller understanding of this option.

6. Promote special offerings more effectively.

"When I talked to you yesterday," Teresa said to Frank, "I really intended to visit more about special offerings. We've only been taking two a year, and that just doesn't seem like enough."

"I agree. Our congregation takes at least fifteen a year."

"That's more than one a month!" Teresa exclaimed. "Don't people complain?"

"Almost never. Someone will sometimes make a joke about it, but people don't really complain. Of course we're careful not to put people on the spot or make them feel that they have to contribute every single time an offering is taken. The amount of promotion we give to an offering depends on how important it is to the overall financial program of the church."

"Well, with only two a year, we can promote both of them as much as we want, and people do give generously to them. I don't know if I want to go to fifteen offerings, but it feels to me like we could have at least half-a-dozen without people feeling pressured. I'd like to know more about what you mean in saying that you promote some more than others."

"If you do two or even six a year, you can put the same emphasis on each one if you want," Frank said. "When you move to a frequency of one a month or more, then you need to think about how to communicate to people in a way that clearly differentiates the ones that are most crucial."

"For example," he continued, "we take an offering that's intended to raise several thousand dollars for a missionary. If we don't raise it, that can have quite a negative impact on that missionary and his family. We do heavy publicity about that in advance, we show a short video in the Sunday school classes on the Sunday preceding the offering, and then we have the appeal made by a person who has recently visited the mission site. We also let people know that we are hoping for a certain number of gifts at the five hundred dollar level and a certain number at the one hundred dollar level. That helps raise expectations. We always meet or exceed the goal for that offering."

"But you don't do a big push with every single offering?"

"Right. Our goals aren't as large for some of the other offerings. Of course we always try to have adequate information to people ahead of time and to make the presentation about the need as interesting and as personalized as we can. Whenever we fail to get any advanced information about a special offering to people, we always see a big drop in the offering. People need to know what's coming and need opportunity to think about what they want to do. That's the opposite of pressure. That's letting people make informed choices. People don't need to be protected from the opportunity to give to important causes. They do occasionally need for us to tell them when a cause is especially important."

Special Offerings

Special offerings have become a more important source of support for many churches in recent years. While a few people may lament too many requests for money, the reality is that the church receives more when it asks more frequently. Most churches don't want to have a special offering every week, but our research shows that monthly special offerings, properly promoted, make a significant difference in the overall giving of the congregation. The following chart shows the percentage of congregations we studied by number of special offerings a year:

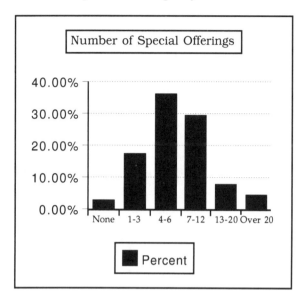

Number of Special Offerings

Percent

Churches with seven to twenty special offerings almost all report larger increases in annual giving than congregations with six or fewer special offerings. Only 4% of the churches we studied had more than twenty special offerings.

Here are some specific item responses we received from the survey of church leaders which was part of the Spirituality and Giving Project:

All special offerings taken in our congregation go to mission needs outside of the congregation. **52.2%** agreed

One or more of the special offerings taken in our congregation goes to help meet the budget of the church or to an area of local church ministry not fully provided for in the budget. **33.5%** agreed

I am satisfied that our special offerings are promoted with the kind of care that maximizes what people are willing to give. **33.9%** agreed

There is a tendency in our church for some people to give more generously to special offerings than to the overall budget of the church. **33.5%** agreed

In interviews with churches, we found that many are going through a transition in terms of the purposes for which special offerings are used. Several churches reported to us that special offerings were once used exclusively for mission needs outside of the congregation, but that is changing. Now they are increasingly using at least some special offerings for needs within the congregation which have not been adequately funded from the budget. As shown in the preceding figures, over half the responding congregations continue to have special offerings exclusively for mission needs outside the congregation, but we sense that percentage is declining. While special offerings will continue to be used heavily for outside needs, there may be greater reliance on them for some internal needs as well.

Only about a third of the church leaders responding to our survey indicated that they feel special offerings are currently promoted with the kind of care needed to maximize response. As we continued to work with churches in the Spirituality and Giving Project, we found that very large improvements are possible in the responses congregations make to special requests. Some important concepts:

- Special offerings should be presented in very positive terms, but people should not be caused to feel guilty for not supporting every special cause which comes. You don't want people to begin lowering their annual pledge or regular giving in anticipation of special offerings! They won't do that unless they are made to feel guilty for not contributing. As long as they feel free to give or not as they feel comfortable, special offerings will not have any negative impact on regular giving to the church. In fact, you will likely see the opposite result. Special offerings can improve the giving habits of people with the result that they are more generous in making annual pledges to the church.

- It's important for people to clearly understand the purpose of a special offering. The more visual the presentation can be, the better. Drama and video can be used during the worship services and/or in classes and groups. Print pieces should also be handed out and/or mailed.

- Clear goals for special offerings are critical, as well as the recognition that not every offering is of equal importance. If you need to raise $5,000 for playground equipment, for example, then say so! Also share something about how many gifts in various categories are needed to achieve the overall goal. Unless given some benchmarks, most members will give the same amount to each special offering.

- Who asks for the money on the day of the special offering makes a difference. If you are collecting money for camp scholarships, then have the request made by children who go to camp – and consider having children take the offering. The pastor can have great influence, but don't have the pastor make the pitch for every special offering.

In his excellent book *44 Ways to Expand the Financial Base of Your Congregation*, Lyle Schaller writes: "Many church leaders assume that if additional money is allocated for one cause or need, some other committee or need will be shortchanged. The evidence suggests this is a completely fallacious assumption. Literally thousands of congregations have experienced a 30 to 100 percent increase in member giving within the space of twelve months without any significant change in the number of contributors" [p.21]. We often fail to have the money we need because we fail to ask for it.

Special offerings trust the judgments of the members and constituents of the church. They make the decision about whether or not to support a given need.

Some churches have used a strategy generally referred to as **Miracle Sunday** for a "special offering" that is truly one-of-a-kind. The goal is to raise a very large sum of money in a single offering on a day called Miracle Sunday. A special committee or task force is generally designated to make the arrangements for that day. Minute speakers, articles in the newsletter, and carefully worded letters to members lead up to Miracle Sunday.

The committee or task force for Miracle Sunday generally includes some persons who

are anticipated to be major contributors to that offering. Having them involved in the process increases the probability of their being extremely generous in that offering.

The letters which lead up to that offering, often between four and seven in number, each provide an important perspective or foundation. One of those letters always makes the financial goal for Miracle Sunday clear and breaks down the contributions needed to achieve the goal. If a congregation wants to raise $100,000 on Miracle Sunday and is likely to have two hundred households represented in worship, the goal should not be expressed as an average gift of $500. It should be made clear that there is a need, for example, for at least two contributions of $10,000; six of $5,000; twelve of $2,000; and twenty of $1,000 – in addition to many between $50 and $1,000. The actual numbers of each level should be determined by careful study in the committee which has been given the Miracle Sunday responsibility.

Another letter in the series could talk about the advanced contributions which have already been received for that offering. This builds confidence and enthusiasm. The persons on the committee who are in a position to make significant gifts are the ones who make this advanced notification possible. The success of Miracle Sunday depends heavily on several people giving out of their accumulated assets rather than out of current income (from savings rather than checking). Refer to the discussion in strategy number five on asset giving. On a Miracle Sunday, 70% – 80% of the total gifts may well come from only 15% – 25% of the people.

Regular Offerings

We should not forget the importance of the regular offering and the role of the offering in the service of worship. Offertory statements, litanies, and prayers should be carefully chosen. You always want to emphasize the spiritual dimension of giving. That can be accomplished through the use of Scripture, through the wording of the prayers, and sometimes through the personal testimony of a member of the congregation.

During the Spirituality and Giving Project, we received a surprising number of inquiries about where the offering should be located in the worship service – especially whether it should come before or after the sermon or homily. The theological stance of your tradition or your own theology may dictate the location. In terms of effectiveness, we are not convinced that the location has any significant impact on how people respond. Some feel that the importance of the offertory can be better emphasized by placing it in a variety of places in the order of service.

In worship services focused on reaching those persons named as seekers, there may be a justifiable argument for not including an offering as part of the service but simply having a place for gifts available at the back of the church. Seekers are persons who often are suspicious that the church is primarily after their money, so the presence of an offertory can be a confirmation of that fear. What must be kept in tension with this, as noted in an earlier chapter, is that in fact the offertory should be part of the act of worship for the mature Christian. We not only give of our material resources during the offertory, but we are also reminded of God's justifiable claim on our time, energy, talents, and love. People who join the church must come to see that sharing our material resources in a joyful and thankful spirit is a central part of the Christian life. Services which are primarily attended by members of the church should always include an offering.

Sample Special Offering Approaches

Because the special offerings chosen by your church will be unique, we cannot provide you with exact wordings to publicize those offerings, but the samples which follow should spark your own creativity.

Summer Scholarships to Camp Simpson

FOR GENERATIONS, summer camp experiences have brought children, youth, and adults closer to nature, to new friends, and to God. Kelli Mett writes about camp: "I liked the night hike and also I liked being away from my parents and not being able to clean my room." Tyler Babcock writes: "I like camp because I get to swim. I liked going in the boat the most." Members of the Junior Class shared:

• "Camp Simpson is a great place to relax and meet new people. The area is beautiful on the lake with the trees. We have morning worship in a spot looking over the lake. It's a great place to see God's creation of nature. The grounds are peaceful and quiet, so you can talk to God easily."

• "What I liked about Camp Simpson was my counselor and my friends. I had a lot of good experiences with them."

• "I think kids should go to camp to have a great time with some really interesting people who also love to praise God."

Because of the tightness in our church budget for the 1996 year, we did not include a line item for help with camp scholarships. The special offering today is for the purpose of providing scholarships for any children or young people in our church who want to go to camp. It costs $75 to provide a partial scholarship to a camper. Some of us who have been especially blessed need to consider making available one or two scholarships ourselves. Others should give as generously as they can toward the provision of scholarships.

Please clearly indicate on one of the pew envelopes that your special gift is for camp scholarships. Only offerings that are clearly marked will go to the scholarship fund. If you are not prepared to give today, you may do so next Sunday. Please give generously to this important ministry!

The above information was inserted (in slightly different form) in the two newsletters which preceded the special offering and was also used as a bulletin insert that day. Children and youth who had been to camp were used as minute speakers the two Sundays preceding the offering. Children and youth were ushers the day of the offering, and a member of the commission responsible for camps made the appeal.

It's also important to thank people for their gifts! The results of the offering were announced in church on the following Sunday by one of the campers. This article appeared in the next church newsletter:

Excellent Camp Offering Response

THANKS to all those who contributed to the offering for camp scholarships on Sunday, March 16, 1997. Because of the tightness of the budget for 1997, we had been forced to remove the $800 line item for camp scholarships from the budget. The special offering was for the purpose of making scholarships available, and a total of $1,395.00 has been received (as of the date of this article). That will make a great difference for several young people this summer. If you have not yet contributed to that offering and would like to do so, gifts can still be made. Any funds received in excess of what is needed for this summer will be reserved to pay future camp or retreat scholarship expenses.

The Finance Commission or other group responsible for each special offering needs to develop a plan for the promotion of that offering. This is especially crucial for those which have very high financial goals relative to the membership of the congregation. One Finance Commission's plan of action for the One Great Hour of Sharing Offering follows:

**One Great Hour of Sharing Offering:
Schedule and Procedures**

Sunday, March 10, 1996:	Banks and Sharing Calendars available at back of the sanctuary. Bulletin announcement.
Sunday, March 17, 1996:	Banks and Sharing Calendars available at back of the sanctuary. Bulletin announcement. Video available for Sunday school classes.
Sunday, March 24, 1996:	Banks and Sharing Calendars available at back of the sanctuary. Bulletin announcement. Video available for Sunday school classes.
Sunday, March 31, 1996:	Bulletin announcement.
Sunday, April 7, 1996:	Bulletin announcement. Brief announcement requested from the pastor about the offering being taken on April 14. Children's sermon refers to One Great Hour needs.
Sunday, April 14, 1996	Bulletin announcement. Brochure/envelope combination inserted in each bulletin. People are encouraged to bring banks to worship. John and Marge make a special appeal for generosity just before the offering, reminding people of target gifts needed to meet the goal. Children invited to bring banks forward as part of the children's sermon, which again links to One Great Hour and to our need to share.

Newsletter article one:

One Great Hour of Sharing Offering
Coming on Sunday, April 14, 1996

The tradition of a One Great Hour of Sharing offering began in 1949. Christians from many different denominations in the United States and Canada pool their resources with overseas partner churches to produce results that change lives. Twenty-one different ministries, located in the United States, Canada, and around the world, will benefit from this offering. Among those ministries are:

- Farming in the Dominican Republic. Over 300 rural communities, in which 43% of the population lives below the poverty level, receive help in improving agricultural production.

- Orphanages in Romania. There are over 120,000 orphaned or abandoned children in Romania, and orphanages are sadly inadequate. Children are often found covered with flies and malnourished. Romanian churches, with funds received from One Great Hour of Sharing, are reaching out to these children, meeting their physical needs and sharing Christ's love.

- Flood Relief in the United States. Floods like those of 1993 damage a tremendous number of homes and crops. One Great Hour of Sharing gifts enable emergency response when such situations arise and also support substantial rebuilding efforts for those without resources.

Many congregations conducted this special offering during March, but our church chose not to do that because of other emphases we had that month. Our special offering will be on Sunday, April 14. In order to meet our goal of $5,000 for this offering, we need at least one gift of $500 and at least ten gifts of $200. All people are encouraged to give generously, perhaps the equivalent of what one spends on a weekend's entertainment.

Newsletter article two:

The Sharing Calendar

On Sunday, March 10, 1996, "Sharing Calendars" and banks were distributed to those households which wanted them, and they continue to be available. The calendar and the bank are used together to put money aside for the One Great Hour of Sharing Offering. Suggestions are made for personal contributions each day for four weeks. Sample

---

suggestions:

- On the first Tuesday on the calendar: Droughts in Senegal left many people without water. Place 2 cents in the bank for every sink, 4 cents for every shower, and 6 cents for every bathtub in your home.

- On the third Saturday on the calendar: In Lebanon, homes are being rebuilt following a bitter civil war. Count the number of doors in your home and place 6 cents in your bank for each one.

Contact the church office if you would like a bank and calendar but did not receive them yet.

Bulletin Announcements:

Sunday, March 10, 1996:

Sharing Calendars and Banks: Our congregation will be taking an offering for One Great Hour of Sharing on Sunday, April 14, 1996. In preparation for that offering, households are invited to use a Sharing Calendar and a bank, which are available at the back of the sanctuary this morning. The Sharing Calendar shares ideas for filling the bank in meaningful ways. The calendar activity for the third Tuesday, for example, says: "In Somalia, thousands of people desperately need medical care. Count the number of items in your medicine cabinet and place two cents for each in your sharing bank." Banks will be presented at worship on April 14. Please, only one bank per household!

Sunday, March 17, 1996:

Sharing Calendars and Banks: Our congregation will be taking an offering for One Great Hour of Sharing on Sunday, April 14, 1996. In preparation for that offering, households are invited to use a Sharing Calendar and a bank, which are again available at the back of the sanctuary this morning.

Sunday, March 24, 1996:

Sharing Calendars and Banks: Sharing Calendars and banks are available at the back of the sanctuary for those persons who have not yet received one. The calendar gives daily activities which help us put money in the bank and understand the depths of human need which some persons experience. Banks will be presented at the One Great Hour of Sharing offering on Sunday, April 14, 1996.

Sunday, March 31, 1996:

Are You Using Your Bank? Many households received Sharing Calendars and banks on March 10, 17 or 24 to be used in preparation for the One Great Hour of Sharing offering. Are you staying current on the suggested activities? The suggested activity for the third Sunday says: "During the floods of 1993, residents of the Midwest watched their houses fill with water room by room. Read *Genesis 7*. Deposit five cents in the bank for each room in your home." Banks and other offerings for One Great Hour of Sharing will be presented on Sunday, April 14, 1996.

Sunday, April 7, 1996:

One Great Hour of Sharing Offering: The One Great Hour of Sharing offering for our congregation will be taken next Sunday, April 14, 1996. Those who have been using the sharing calendar and bank over the last few weeks should bring the bank to worship services that day. If you are not going to be present on April 14 and want to leave a special offering today, feel free to do so – use one of the pew envelopes and clearly indicate that the gift is for One Great Hour of Sharing.

Sunday, April 14, 1996:

One Great Hour of Sharing Offering: A special combined brochure and offering envelope for One Great Hour of Sharing are enclosed in the bulletin this morning. If your household used the Sharing Calendar and bank approach the last several weeks, you can present the bank this morning. The offering goes to meet deep human needs in the United States and around the world. Please give generously to the One Great Hour of Sharing offering – we need at least one gift of $500 and at least ten gifts of $200. Consider taking as your own standard the amount of money normally spent on entertainment on a weekend or during a week.

Newsletter article following the offering:

One Great Hour of Sharing Offering Raises $6,100 ! !

Our goal for this offering was $5,000, and we went over that goal by $1,100, which will make a great difference for human need! Over a hundred households used the special banks that were provided, and there were several generous special contributions. Twenty-one different ministries, located in the United States, Canada, and around the world, benefit from this offering. Thanks so much for your commitment to Christ and the church! If you wanted to contribute but were not prepared to give last week, the offering is still open – just mail a check to the church or put it in the offering this week, clearly marking your gift for "One Great Hour of Sharing."

An announcement of the results was also made by the Finance Chairperson on the following Sunday. Members of the Missions Commission wrote personal notes to all those on record as having made gifts to this offering.

One congregation, deeply concerned about the availability of money to help transients and the homeless who turned to the church, had special offering envelopes printed with the form shown below in a bright red color on a pink background. A supply of the envelopes is continually available in the pew racks where the bright color makes them stand out, and the pastor or a member of the Social Concerns Commission lifts up the need every quarter. It is rare for a week to go by without at least a few people using one of the envelopes to make a special gift.

Social Action Emergency Fund
Offering

Name: _____

Address: _____

_____

Try having some fun in the promotion of a special need in your church. One congregation calling a new pastor needed to raise $10,000 for the moving expenses to get that person and family from one side of the country to the other.

They considered the possibility of inviting people to pledge so many dollars for each mile of the trip, but then they considered the fact that the new minister would literally be moving across the country. The $10,000 goal worked out to an even $200 a state for the fifty states. They decided to give members of the congregation opportunity to acquire a "deed" to a state for each $200 gift. The congregation had about a hundred giving units, so they encouraged some to acquire multiple states, knowing that others would need to make smaller donations.

They followed this calendar:

2nd Sunday in September: Campaign announcement.

2nd Week in September: Letter, information sheet, and pledge form mailed to each household.

3rd and 4th Sundays in September: Updates on progress announced at church. Maps posted with states which had been "acquired" colored by children's classes.

5th Sunday in September: Final date for pledges for this special campaign to be submitted.

The campaign was oversubscribed by more than two thousand dollars. The pages which follow share the basic materials used in the mailing for that campaign.

Park Street Church

September 10, 1996

TO: Members and Friends of Park Street Church

At the time the board and the congregation passed the budget for 1996, we were aware that a separate fund-raising drive would be necessary to take care of expenses related to the new pastor's move and to the beginning of his ministry.

We're all pleased that Adam Watson begins as our new pastor in November. He and his wife Helen will be moving from California – a considerable distance. We need $10,000.00 to pay for the move and for some minor improvement to the parsonage. The enclosed information sheet gives more detailed information about those needs.

We decided to call this special emphasis the "Move Across the Country Fund" since we are literally moving Adam and Helen across the country. The $10,000 breaks down into $200 a state for the fifty states. As a way of having fun with the money-raising process, we are offering you and your family the opportunity to "purchase" one or more of the fifty states. Why not buy your favorite state or states? We'll color states on maps posted around the church to show our progress on the goal. Whether you purchase the whole eastern seaboard or a small part of Michigan, we'll send you a certificate for each state that you acquire or those toward which you contribute. Donations of all sizes are important.

Please prayerfully consider what you can do to help our church with this important need. Any money raised in excess of the needs for this fund will be used for capital improvements in the church or parsonage.

Sincerely,

Mary Taylor
For the Stewardship Commission

Move Across the Country Fund

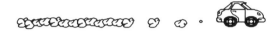

Why the fund has been established: At the time our congregation approved the budget for 1996, we were aware that there would be extra expenses involved with the calling of a new pastor. Because we did not know what the magnitude of those expenses would be, we determined that we would conduct a separate financial drive to raise that money when the time came. Now that our congregation has called Adam to come as our new pastor, effective November 1, 1996, it's time for us to raise the necessary funds. Adam and Helen come to us from California, so they are literally moving across the country.

What the fund covers: The fund covers the two major, unbudgeted expenses connected with Adam's move and ministry:

To move Adam and Helen across the country.	$5,500.00
To install new carpeting on the main floor of the parsonage, replace the garage door, and purchase a new refrigerator.	4,500.00
Total	$10,000.00

The cost of the move alone by a commercial moving company would normally be in the range of nine to ten thousand dollars. We are fortunate that we have secured a bid of $4,750 for that move; an additional $750 has been allocated to pay the costs for Adam and Helen's trip separate from the moving van. The $5,500 pays all the direct moving expenses.

We have also known for more than a year that we needed to make some improvements in the parsonage, and we want to do that as part of our welcome to Adam and Helen. All the carpeting on the main floor needs to be replaced, and it will be far easier to accomplish that before Adam and Helen's furniture has arrived. We also need a new garage door and a new refrigerator.

Buy a State: Since this is literally a move across the country, the planning committee decided that an interesting way to handle the fund-raising would be to give members and friends of the congregation opportunity to acquire one or more of the fifty states through their donation to the Move Across the Country Fund. The $10,000 needed breaks down into $200 for each of the fifty states. Based on our congregational giving patterns, it will be important for some of us to purchase more than one state. We need:

- At least three individuals or families who will purchase at least four states. (A $800 donation or more)
- At least four individuals or families who will purchase at least three states. (A $600 donation or more)
- Many individuals and families who will purchase one or two states. ($200 to $400 donations)
- Many individuals and families who will contribute to the cost of purchasing a state. (Donations of any size)

In other words, donations of all sizes are wanted and needed. We won't manage to cover the map unless some of our households acquire multiple states, but we also recognize that $200 may be too large a gift for some. Gifts do not have to be given in a lump sum. They can be given on a weekly or a monthly basis in September, October, and November. *Please prayerfully consider what you can do to help.*

Sunday, September 29: We would like to receive all intention of giving forms for this special fund drive by the worship service on Sunday, September 29. You may bring your intention of giving form to church on any Sunday in September, or send it to the church office.

Updates: Maps will be posted around the church with states colored on a weekly basis to show the progress on our $10,000.00 goal. We'll also share updates in the bulletin each week. Individuals and families will be notified of the states or states which they have acquired or to which they have contributed. Wouldn't you like to own New York State? Or the State of California? What about Hawaii? Or Alaska? And yes, someone will have to take New Jersey!*

If you have questions about this special fund drive, feel free to contact Don West, the chairperson of the Move Across the Country Task Force.

Our apologies to the people of New Jersey!

Which state or states would you like?

✂ -

Move Across the Country Fund • Intention of Giving

Name(s): _____

Yes, I/we want to help our new pastor move across the country and to help make the needed improvements in the parsonage. Through our donation, we'd like to acquire (check one and fill in blanks as appropriate):

_____ One state for a donation of $200.00
_____ Two states for a donation of $400.00
_____ Three states for a donation of $600.00
_____ Four states for a donation of $800.00
_____ _____ states for a donation of _____ ($200 a state)
_____ A portion of a state for a donation of _____ (any amount you wish)

I/we plan to make this donation in this way (check one and fill in blanks as appropriate):

_____ Check enclosed or attached.
_____ By three monthly gifts (September, October, and November).
_____ By ten weekly gifts (September 29 through December 1).
_____ Other (please specify): _____

Just for Fun! Please feel free to list any preferences you have for the states you want to acquire or to help acquire:

_____

_____

Fund-Raising Activities

Virtually all congregations have at least some special fund-raising activities like ice cream socials, bazaars, pancake suppers, Christmas tree sales, and similar events. They are often sponsored by a specific class or group in the church to raise money for the activities of that class or group, but sometimes they are sponsored by the congregation as a whole. Some churches use these activities to raise money for the budget. While there are some exceptions, in general the smaller the congregation, the more likely that some of the budget will be raised through a fund-raising activity in addition to that which comes through pledges and offerings. Survey responses concerning fund-raising activities:

Our church has some fund-raising activities (like ice cream socials, bazaars, pancake suppers, etc.) which help support the budget of the church. **28.3%** agreed

Our church has some fund-raising activities (like ice cream socials, bazaars, pancake suppers, etc.) which help support specific needs in our church or in missions. **70.4%** agreed

Fund-raising activities are one of the ways that we are able to increase the number of persons who help support the financial needs of the church. **84.6%** agreed

Our reporting and discussion concerning fund-raising activities is being placed in the special offerings section of this report, because those activities are so often done to raise money for a specific cause rather than for the general budget of the church.

Some fund-raising authorities speak negatively about the use of fund-raising activities like pancake suppers and bazaars to generate money for the basic budget of the church. There is an understandable concern that if people are putting great energy into fund-raising activities that they may feel they have done their part and do not need to pledge as generously to the budget of the church.

For the most part, however, our research does not support that conclusion. We did not find a significant difference in average pledging or giving amounts between congregations which relied in part on fund-raising activities for the general budget and those which did not. The typical church which we found using fund-raising activities to raise money for the general budget had fewer than three hundred members and was endeavoring to support a fairly substantial budget relative to the size of the congregation.

The leadership in those fund-raising activities was sometimes taken by a particular group in the church, like the women's group or a Sunday school class, with everyone invited to help in a variety of ways. When the events have become community traditions, the amounts raised can sometimes be substantial relative to the budget of the church. We encountered a congregation near a Big Ten university which serves chicken dinners to people on the way to football games – annually raising $10,000 of a $70,000 budget through five or six dinners. We visited with people in a rural congregation which has an annual bazaar that raises $4,000 against a church budget of $45,000.

The majority of fund-raising activities, of course, are to raise money for specific programs or mission needs rather than for the general budget of the church. Most of these activities are sponsored by a class or group within the church. The classic examples are fund-raising for youth summer trips, for the renovation of a Sunday school classroom, and for a mission project.

As already shared, 84.6% of the church leaders responding feel that these activities help involve more people. Individuals who have not been highly active in the church and who have not been significant givers often find it meaningful to be involved in such activities. Working with others in the church and learning more about the needs to which the church responds can help motivate people to higher levels of giving.

When looking at church finances and at the congregation, it's important to stay mindful of the reality that people are at different levels in the maturity of their giving and in the financial resources from which they can give. There need to be a variety of ways in which people can contribute to the church, and fund-raising activities may be the "port of entry" to the giving program for some individuals. At the same time, it is also important to remember that the development of the spiritual life should result in people feeling good about giving from their income and their assets as well as through fund-raising projects.

If your congregation is in financial trouble, having more fund-raising activities is not likely to be the solution to that trouble. On the other hand, fund-raising activities can provide a means to increase giving to specific causes and can broaden the base of participation.

7. Encourage the pastor to be actively involved in stewardship education and fund-raising.

"Exactly how does it help you as a pastor to have information about the giving of your members?" Teresa asked Frank. She, Frank, and Jim were meeting again – this time for the specific purpose of discussing church finances.

"Let me share a few examples. I have a member who owns his own construction company, lives in a home that has to have set him back over three hundred thousand and drives a Mercedes. This man was giving the church twenty-five hundred a year. Now that's not a bad pledge, but it's not much relative to what he has to be earning. I'd never confront him directly about his giving. What I did instead was when I had a special need for help on a project, I called him up myself, explained the need to him, and asked if he could give us two thousand to complete it. I knew that wasn't asking for too much; and because the request came directly from me, he did it. Then I got him more involved in the financial campaign so that he learned more about the needs of the church and got an idea that some people were far more generous than he had been. He moved his giving to a hundred a week the next year, and now he's up to twenty thousand a year. I never confronted him, but knowing that he needed encouragement made it possible for me to

work with him."

"Here's another example," he continued. "I was very surprised in looking at giving figures the first time to see that a social worker and a school teacher, a husband and wife, were giving the church two hundred a week. I know what they earn, and that has to be more than a tithe of their income. I got one of them pulled into the stewardship commission, and I asked one of them to be a minute speaker on our financial campaign the next fall. Both of them have done a lot to further the stewardship program. They give out of a deep spirituality, and they're pretty good at communicating that to others."

"But you never directly addressed the level of their giving with them, right?" Jim asked.

"That's right. Simply having the information was enough for me to act. That way people aren't made overly conscious of my having access to the information. I doubt that anyone in our church thinks anything about my having that access."

"I do remember one time," Teresa offered, "when the treasurer suggested to me that I might consider calling on a particular family. It turns out that the husband had lost his job, and the family was going through a very hard time spiritually as a result. I'm assuming the treasurer told me that because their giving was down, but I've never known for sure."

"Not knowing about that kind of need is one of my concerns," Jim said. "A drop in attendance or a drop-off in giving are the two ways you most readily know someone is having personal problems or is upset with the church. If they stop coming, there are people who miss them; and the attendance records reflect that. If they stop giving, the church treasurer or financial secretary may be the only person who knows. You can't respond to something if you don't know about it. I worry about what opportunities for ministry I'm missing by not knowing about the giving patterns of people."

"That," agreed Frank, "is the best reason of all for the pastor having access to the church's financial records. Of course access to those records is only part of the way the pastor needs to interact with the church's financial program."

"But in my church people get very uncomfortable if the pastor gives the impression of being concerned about money," said Teresa.

"You always must be careful," Frank said, "that you don't give the impression that the money is more important than the people. My experience, however, is that most people are okay with the pastor talking about money unless the pastor just beats the topic to death. After all, the pastor knows more about the theology of giving than anyone else."

"Or at least we should," Jim said. "The truth is that my seminary education didn't teach me much about stewardship education or about church finances. I've had to figure out most of that on my own and by reading. My problem, I think, is that I get too apologetic when I try to talk about money. I say something like: 'Well, you really don't want to hear this, and I really don't want to say this, but it's time for us to think about our giving again.' With that kind of introduction, no wonder people turn me off."

"I do the same thing," Teresa offered. "I even find it awkward to be talking about giving with the two of you. No wonder I don't feel good about discussing it with people in the church. Yet what Frank is saying makes sense."

"When I went to seminary," Jim said, "it was popular to say that if you gave good pastoral care and good sermons, then the rest would take care of itself – people would come and people would give. I don't know if that was ever true, but it sure isn't true now. Increased attendance and increased giving don't come by accident. You have to be intentional about your strategies, and you have to help people be intentional about their response to the church and to the call of Christ."

"When I first started out in the ministry," Frank said, "I didn't talk about money at all. Then one year the chairperson of the financial drive for my church said to me, 'Frank, are you trying to sabotage the financial campaign?' I told him, 'Of course not. What do you mean?' And he explained to me that my saying nothing at all about the financial campaign gave people the impression that I didn't think it was important. I was sending out the wrong

message without intending to do it. You just can't escape the need for the pastor to be actively involved in church finances."

The Pastor and Church Finances

Many pastors are uncomfortable dealing with the financial aspects of the church, and some churches don't like the idea of the pastor knowing what individual members give. It's very difficult, however, to have effective stewardship education or fund-raising without the pastor being part of the process. For example:

- The pastor has the major leadership role in the church. If he or she doesn't clearly communicate that giving is important, many members will conclude that it isn't. The steward-ship program of the church shouldn't be conducted in a vacuum from which the pastor is removed. Stewardship is important both in terms of the financial health of the church and in terms of the spiritual health of the congregation.

- If the pastor is apologetic about asking people to share their financial resources, many members will conclude there is something presumptuous about those persons who are more direct in their approach. If the pastor models a polite but direct approach, others will follow that model. People respond well to a polite and direct approach – they are resistive to an apologetic approach. The research done in the Spirituality and Giving Project makes it clear that most active church members do feel they should give more to the church and would feel better about themselves if they did.

  For the most part, people only respond negatively to the pastor's involvement in the stewardship program when the pastor himself or herself is overly apologetic or when the pastor exhibits such a preoccupation with finances that it appears money really is more important than people. Most pastors are in no danger of communicating that impression.

- The pastor has the best biblical and theological background in most churches and needs to have a major role in stewardship education from the pulpit and in other settings. An annual stewardship sermon (given in 97% of the churches we surveyed) isn't enough. In fact, some pastors might do well to abandon the concept of an annual stewardship sermon and instead to refer to stewardship issues in sermons throughout the year, using some of the many good biblical texts available on stewardship and related issues. The emphasis doesn't have to continually be on asking for money – stewardship education involves more than that. Areas of concern include:

  - The example we set for our children in stewardship.

  - How we spend our money.

  - Whom we view as the source of all we have.

  - The kind of power money tends to exert over us and over others.

  - The reality that when we give generously to others, we seem to establish an openness which makes it easier for us to receive. [See especially 2 Corinthians 9.]

  - What it means to live with a continuing spirit of thanksgiving and an awareness of the countless blessings God has given us.

  - The Genesis view of creation and our responsibilities and opportunities to work with God as the creative process continues.

  - The responsibility we have as stewards for the natural world.

  - The connecting nature of the body of Christ and our bonds with other congregations, including the place of shared ministries.

  - The importance of outreach to the poor of the world; the clear call of Christ for the church to

    care "about the least of these."

  - The tremendously broadened definition of one's neighbor which Jesus communicated in the Parable of the Good Samaritan and by his actions.

- It's very difficult to develop a tithing congregation if the pastor doesn't tithe and talk about tithing. *Some congregations need to reexamine their compensation structure to be sure the pastor is being paid well enough that tithing is a realistic possibility.* Think about the reference groups used in your church in evaluating pastoral salaries. Most pastors have a three- or four-year graduate degree on top of an undergraduate degree. Does your church pay what an educator with that much advance training would receive from a public school or a college? What an attorney would receive? Does your church provide adequate reimbursement of the expenses incurred by your pastor – including the high automobile expense which most pastors have in the course of their work?

- The pastor has an important role in the planning of the annual campaign, particularly in regard to emphasizing the spiritual dimension of giving. Some of the issues of strategy which every campaign committee faces are in fact theological issues, and the guidance of the pastor is important. The success of a campaign also depends, to a sometimes significant extent, on the pastor communicating the importance of the campaign to the congregation.

- In the process of regular pastoral work, the pastor has many unique opportunities to encourage special gifts and to help people think about their wills, living trusts, endowments, etc. There may be times when the pastor will initiate a contact and then ask the finance committee to follow up.

- The pastor is almost always involved in the orientation of new members. It's important for that process to include an emphasis on stewardship.

- The giving of members is an important indicator of their spiritual health and of the health of the congregation. Pastors who have that information are in a better position to help individuals and the church. A poor atmosphere for commitment of material gifts generally reflects leadership problems and spiritual problems. The pastor must play a major role in addressing those difficulties.

- The pastor needs to take the initiative in creating a climate in which people become comfortable talking about the relationship between money and the Christian life.

Think Positive

People will respond negatively to the pastor or to anyone else in the church if finances are approached from a perspective of manipulation and guilt or with the implication that what a person gives is more important than who a person is. People need help in cultivating generous hearts – not guilty hearts.

Guilt may work in the short-term, but it generally does not work for the long-term. Guilt is only helpful to most of us in showing us the disparity between what we are doing and what we are capable of doing – a more positive attitude is required to bridge that gap. The pastor is the one in the best position to keep people focused on the positive aspects of giving and on the importance of giving to the spiritual life.

8. Send more frequent financial statements to members and constituents who support the church.

"How often do you send statements to members and other givers?" Jim asked Frank.

"We've been doing it monthly for the last two years. Our office staff and volunteers groaned when we first started doing it, but I think it's helped us in at least two ways. First, it helps people get off to a good start on their giving. When we did quarterly statements, people would be three months behind before they got a statement reminding them. Now they find out at the end of any given month. It's a lot easier to make up for being a month behind than for three months. Second, we include information each month that helps people know how the church is doing financially or that encourages them to give to special needs. There's evidence that people read that information and respond. Our giving to special needs has gone up considerably since we started doing the monthly statements and information."

"Our church just does them annually," Jim

said. "We had been doing them quarterly, but we cut back some on office help. Then people started asking if the statements really made any difference."

"The quarterly statements sure make a difference for us," Teresa said. Whenever the statements are mailed out, we tend to get an influx of money the next week. People find out that they're behind, and they give extra to catch up."

"That's part of the reason that going to monthly statements helps," said Frank. "People are used to monthly bills for electricity, water, the telephone, and credit cards. Some people give so automatically every week or month that their statements simply show them paid up, but there are many others who don't even give until they receive the statement. Sending those out monthly is one of the easiest ways I know of to encourage giving. There are even offering envelope systems now which let you mail out the envelopes a month at a time rather than giving a year's supply to people. That mailing can be a regular reminder of the importance of giving, and the the envelopes for the coming month can be sent with a monthly statement of giving."

"We only do the statements quarterly, but our treasurer always writes a letter about the church," said Teresa. "One of the things she expresses on a regular basis is thanksgiving for what people are doing and giving. It's easy to start taking peoples' gifts for granted. We need to thank people."

"Amen to that," said Frank. "We always have a letter signed by the treasurer or the financial secretary which is sent to all people who make pledges. When we have special offerings, we also try to have notes of appreciation sent to the people who give. People need to feel that their gifts are making a difference and are appreciated."

Frequent Statements

Almost all churches responding to our surveys provide an annual statement to givers, and 74% of those responding to our survey provide quarterly statements. Only 7.8%, however, send statements on a monthly basis. All of the churches which changed to monthly statements have had giving increase. Most churches which send monthly statements use that as an opportunity to enclose information about the church's financial situation and about any special needs. The frequent statements help people avoid getting too far behind in their giving, and the information on needs motivates some persons to give beyond their regular pledge or pattern of support.

This strategy is especially effective and helpful when a high percentage of households (10% or more) finish each year with pledges unpaid. People's intentions are generally good, but they can get so far behind that there is no opportunity for them to catch up in their giving.

The monthly letter provides significant help to people in understanding the needs of the church. Those letters can also encourage gifts to special causes, and including a return envelope with the letter can be a way of encouraging gifts to a special cause (or the opportunity to catch up on one's pledge or intention of giving).

The smallest increases in those churches sending monthly statements came in Anabaptist congregations (Church of the Brethren, Brethren, and Mennonite congregations) with very high percentages of persons who tithe. Congregations which did not enclose information about the church's financial situation or about special needs also did not see large increases. Some churches send the statements by mail; others handed out most of them to persons as they arrived for worship services or used a congregational mail-box system.

People also respond more positively to hand-addressed statements and letters than to those which have computer labels! For a large congregation, the task of hand-addressing a large number of statements each month may seem overwhelming and may not be worth the effort. Computer hardware and software systems which permit envelopes to be laser-addressed rather than done with labels are one way of helping on the strategy. Many laser printers produce so much heat that envelopes are difficult to run through them in any quantity, but there are some brands which are designed to handle envelopes without melting the glue – and some kinds of envelope stock which work better. If you need

suggestions in either of those areas, drop a note to us at Christian Community [6404 S. Calhoun Street, Fort Wayne, Indiana 46807] and we'll send you some names.

Hand-written addresses do have sufficient power that they should be considered when information being mailed with the financial statements reveals a critical financial situation for the congregation.

Notes on the Fiscal Year and the Annual Campaign

Another strategy can be to actually change the fiscal year of the congregation. Going from January 1 through December 31 to July 1 through June 30 may result in significant improvements. Spring can be a time of optimism – a good time to seek new pledges. If people catch up on their giving at the end of the fiscal year in June (rather than December on a January 1 through December 31 fiscal year), that will produce extra cash to move through the summer season. [There was a period of time when church leaders worried that the burden of extra taxes would make people unwilling to pledge generously in the spring. Now the numbers of people receiving tax refunds is so large that pledging in the spring may be a very sound strategy.]

Some persons ask about the wisdom of an annual campaign and the making of pledges if giving needs to be emphasized throughout the year. Those who pledge give, on the average, twice as much as those who do not. Those who pledge a percentage of their income, whether that percentage is a tithe or not, give three times as much on average as those who do not pledge.

Teresa and Frank are right when they say that it's important to thank people for their gifts. Only 47% of the churches responding to our congregational survey indicated that they have a clear strategy to see that people are thanked for their pledges and other giving to the church. On surveys of individual members, however, we repeatedly see reflected the desire of people to feel that their gifts are appreciated and make a difference. In interviews, many people told us of significant gifts which were received in response to the extension of thanks for gifts already received.

Avoid Gloom and Doom

In providing regular financial updates, you want to speak frankly about the needs of the church. Be careful, however, not to paint a picture which is unnecessarily gloomy.

Many churches have become accustomed to reports in the bulletin and in newsletters which list:

Average weekly amount needed:	$ 5,500.00	(for example)
Amount received last week:	$ 4,955.00	
Over (under) needed amount:	($ 545.00)	

For many congregations, the reality is that the average amount received is less than the average amount needed almost every week. There are many churches in which a substantial portion of the total giving for the year is not received until the last three months of the year. In most of these situations, church treasurers, financial secretaries, and other leaders have learned how to spread out expenditures to take into consideration the variable cash flow or have learned to carry forward some balance from the preceding year.

People often think that printing the information that average weekly receipts are not sufficient will motivate people to give more. Over the years, however, persons who read the bulletin and newsletter become accustomed to seeing those negative reports and cease to be motivated by them. Visitors and prospective members, however, are not accustomed to reading those reports and are likely to be scared by them – becoming uncertain about whether or not they want to join a church which appears to be in serious financial trouble.

Information about problems in church giving belong in letters that accompany statements or should be communicated in some way other than the bulletin and the newsletter. In general, though you want to frankly address tight money situations, the overall tone of financial communications needs to be positive and upbeat.

Sample Letters

The pages which follow contain examples of letters which have been included with the financial statements sent to church members and constituents.

October 16, 1996

Dear First Church Friends,

Your statement of giving through the third quarter of 1996 is enclosed with this letter. In the first three quarters of the year, our church has received a total of $139,164 in giving. That figure represents 71.5% of our 1996 budget of $194,730.

Most members are on target with their pledges, and that commitment means a great deal to the church. If giving for the fourth quarter reflects the same proportion of our budget needs as it did last year and if the commissions continue to be conservative in their expenditures, we should be able to finish the year in the black.

Please continue to support our church with your prayers and attendance as well as with your financial gifts. As we move toward the Thanksgiving and Christmas seasons, there are many opportunities to deepen our faith.

With appreciation for your involvement in First Church,

Sincerely,

Charles Sommerville
Financial Secretary

January 19, 1997

Dear <Name entered by word processor>,

Your statement of giving through the fourth quarter of 1996 is enclosed with this letter. Thanks to the extremely high proportion of members who paid their pledges in full and to the responsible handling of expenditures by commissions, we finished the year in the black and were able to make an additional donation of $3,000 to the Church United Food Pantry.

The church also received generous gifts for the Heifer Project offering, which was an emphasis in both the Sunday school and worship, and for the Christmas eve offering which was for the emergency needs of our congregation's members and friends.

Our goal for the Heifer Project had been $4,000, and we actually raised $5,344! The Christmas Eve offering brought $2,050. Since the emergency needs of our congregation's members and friends can't always be anticipated, we continually are at work raising money for that fund. If you didn't have an opportunity to contribute on Christmas eve, please remember that it isn't too late!

Your continued support of the church through your financial gifts, your attendance, your service, and your prayers will again be important in 1997.

Best wishes for a new year filled with blessings.

Sincerely,

Marilyn Lopez
Treasurer

October 16, 1996

Mr. and Mrs. <Word processor supplied>
2215 N. <Street Name>
<City>, <State> <Zip>

Dear XXXXXXXXX and XXXXXXXXXXX,

Finances will be tight for the last part of 1996. There's just no other way to say it. As your Stewardship Commission has examined the third quarter financial situation for our church, it's clear that we face a potential shortfall of $50,000. The Stewardship Commission will do everything possible to control expenses, but there is little fat in the 1996 budget, which was only 2% more than 1995.

There are several reasons for the financial squeeze, especially the retirement, relocation, change in circumstances, or death of some deeply committed, life-long members of our congregation. This underscores our need to do better outreach for new members, but it also emphasizes the need for us to examine our own levels of giving.

Your intention of giving to the congregation for 1996 and your actual giving are only known to the treasurer, Sara Adams, and the assistant treasurer, Ruth Watson. Your current statement of giving has been inserted with this letter by one of them. Depending on your own financial situation, please consider:

- If you are current on your intention of giving for 1996, as the majority of our members are, THANKS. Your staying on target for the rest of the year helps us in our planning. If we are going to finish the year in the black, however, those of us who have good incomes need to prayerfully consider additional giving beyond our pledges for the fourth quarter. At least twenty-five of us need to give an additional $1,000 each in addition to the many other extra gifts which will be received.

- If circumstances have kept you from being able to stay current on your pledge, remember that what you give during the last quarter can still make a great difference for our own church programs and for the other ministries we support. Even if it isn't realistic to make up for the first part of the year, simply beginning to make regular gifts between now and the end of the year will be a help to the church and will help you and the church move into 1997 in a positive, enthusiastic way.

- If you are starting to do end-of-the-year tax planning, consider making a gift of appreciated assets to the church. For example, you may have stocks, bonds, real estate, or a life insurance policy which has gained considerably in value from the time of purchase. Depending on your specific financial circumstances, you may be able to make a gift of that asset to the church, claim its current value as a charitable income tax deduction, and avoid capital gains tax on the increased value. Call Max Clark for more information on this possibility.

Thank you for your careful attention to this letter and for your prayers for our congregation.

Sincerely,

Max Clark, Chairman
John Taylor, Secretary
For The Stewardship
Commission

March 10, 1997

TO: Members and Friends of Park Avenue Church

By the time we've paid taxes, paid the costs of housing, paid for groceries, paid our transportation expenses, paid the insurance bills, and taken care of other inescapable costs of living, it doesn't feel as though we can stretch the remaining money far enough to do the things we want.

Park Avenue Church continues to be thankful that so many people, in the midst of other financial pressures, place top priority on what they give to Christ's work through the church. Many of us have learned that when we truly put God first, everything else works out better. Our giving does make a difference for the many people served by our church and by organizations such as Crestview and Windsor College which receive congregational support.

Your record of giving through February is enclosed. If you have not yet made a pledge or intention of giving for 1997, it is not too late to do so; just call the church office.

Many of you have noticed the extensive work being done to the ceiling and the lighting in the church foyer and in the men's restroom on the first floor. That work certainly improves the appearance of our church. The extent of the cost of those repairs was not anticipated by the Stewardship Commission at the time the 1997 budget was developed. The final cost will be around $8,000, which must be paid from a line item budget of $10,000, leaving relatively little reserve should similar repairs need to be made later in the 1997 year. No special offering has been taken for this project, but gifts from those who would like to help would certainly be appreciated! If you wish to help with the expense of those improvements, please write "ceiling project" on your check.

Speaking of special offerings, we received over a thousand dollars for One Great Hour of Sharing! That's a significant cause for celebration since so many vital ministries are supported by that offering.

Sincerely,

Barb Wallace
Treasurer

February 5, 1997

TO: Members and Friends of First Church

Our past practice at First Church of Adams County has been to provide quarterly statements of giving. This year we are providing an additional statement which shares contributions just for January. Your January record of giving is enclosed.

If you have not yet made a pledge or intention of giving for 1997, it is not too late to do so; just call the church office. If you should be running slightly behind the level of giving which you want to maintain, this would be an ideal time to increase your contributions.

The information at the bottom of this page may be of interest to you. Our giving to the church and to other worthy causes should flow from our thankfulness for what God has provided in our lives. Your gifts to First Church make a significant difference in the witness our church is able to have in this community and in the world.

Sincerely,

Bob Bennett
Treasurer

How Do We Feel about Money?

Certainly all of us want to stretch our dollars as far as we can, but how do we feel about the money we have and spend? A recent survey by Louis Harris and Associates shares some interesting perspectives:

- Almost two-thirds of Americans earning less than $50,000 a year agreed with Christ's statement: "You cannot serve both God and money." Among those earning over $50,000 a year, only 47% agreed.

- Over eighty percent of Americans have given God thanks for their financial well-being. The more people have, however, the less likely they are to have shared their thanks with God.

- Over three-fourths of those with lower incomes ($25,000 a year or less) agreed that the love of money is the root of evil. Only half of higher income respondents agreed with that statement.

- How many pray for guidance in using money? Sixty percent of those earning $25,000 a year or less; forty percent of those earning $50,000 a year or more.

RELAX! What's enclosed is definitely not a bill.

February 16, 1997

Most of us feel swamped with mail that we would rather not have received: politicians telling us that a vote for them will solve our problems (NOT LIKELY!), advertisements for all sorts of things that we don't especially want to buy, and bills for products and services we've already utilized.

Your financial statement from St. Matthew's Church for the first month of the new year is enclosed. Our church financial statements are definitely not bills! Our church giving is voluntary, in response to our thankfulness for the blessings God has given us. The statement of giving is in fact a "thank you" from the church.

So relax – but don't relax too much! Our average weekly giving for the first six Sundays of 1996 is $8,473, which is $1,200 a week less than our current obligations. We normally do run a little low in the first quarter of the year and intentionally carry forward a balance to compensate for that, but it's a reminder of the need to be as regular in our giving as possible.

If you have not yet made a pledge for 1997, it is not too late to do so; just call the church office. If you are running slightly behind the level of giving which you want to maintain, this would be an ideal time to increase your contributions.

Although we certainly aren't ready to run it on Sunday morning, we can celebrate the fact that the air conditioning system approved at our December congregational meeting has now been installed. Most of the expense of that system is covered by designated contributions, but we still need another $2,000 to pay the installation bill. If you feel good about our sanctuary being cooler in the summer, now would be a good time for you to express that with an extra gift!

With appreciation for your commitment to our church,

Jenna Kellogg
Treasurer

July 21, 1996

Dear Friends of Forest Hill Church,

The year is already half over and our church financial secretary has prepared the second quarter giving statements. Yours is enclosed.

Here's an overview of our financial situation in the general fund as of June 30, 1996:

	Year-to-Date June 30, 1996	Year-to-Date June 30, 1995
Receipts	$198,734	$178,021
Expenses	$208,296	$189,792

The general fund functions like a household checking account with offerings and other income deposited and checks written for expenses. We began the year with a balance of $24,260 in that fund. Without that balance, we would be in the red. As you can see, however, that same pattern in giving was true last year. We normally receive a larger portion of our pledge income during the second half of the year. Overall our giving is up, and your generosity makes a difference in what we can accomplish as a church. This year's budget includes our new part-time youth director and higher giving to missions.

I hope that you are among those who have been enjoying our newly paved parking lot this summer. It's also good to see that our special summer children's program continues to provide creative activities for the children to enjoy. Your gifts have helped make those and many other improvements and programs possible.

The Stewardship Commission expresses appreciation to all those who have given generously and consistently to the church.

Sincerely yours,

Tracey Cunningham
Treasurer

P.S. $10,000 is still needed to complete the payment for the new parking lot. If you would like to give something extra this summer, that would be a helpful designation. Any money received above the $10,000 needed will be used for other capital improvements.

Thanksgiving will be here soon!

I feel thankful for many things – including the fact that I'm not a turkey. The turkeys are safe from my household, which will be eating vegetarian out of respect to our daughters, who are more enlightened than their parents. Whatever you'll be eating on Thanksgiving day, I hope this season of the year carries many blessings for you.

Your giving statement through the end of October, 1996, is enclosed with this letter. I'm pleased to report that over ninety percent of our members and friends are on target with their pledges to the Current Expense Fund, to the Building Fund, and to the World Mission Fund. We're ten months into the fiscal year; and if everyone gave in even installments throughout the year, we should be at 83% of our pledge goals to all those funds. We're very close!

Fund	Dollars Received	Percent of Annual Goal
Current Expense Fund	$704,375	80.75%
Building Fund	635,630	79.42%
World Mission Fund	633,150	72.36%

Given that some of our members always give a larger amount on their pledges in the last two months of the year, we should be on target for the Current Expense Fund and for the Building Fund. The World Mission Fund, however, is of some concern to me and to the Stewardship Education Committee. You'll remember that our goal for the year was to give as much to others as we spent on current expenses for ourselves. We need to pick up the pace of our giving if we're going to meet that goal.

Your giving does make a difference! Your giving changes lives in our church, our community, and in the world. In my thanksgiving prayers, I think of your generosity and pray for God's blessings to touch your lives.

In His Service,
Ross Matthews, Financial Secretary

9. Emphasize the mission and vision of your church rather than the line item budget – and remember that people give to people and God, not budgets.

"Well, no one gives money to a calculator – and most people don't give money to the line items of a budget," Brad said to Mary as they visited in his office. He had just used the small calculator on his desk to run some figures on budget projections for the new year. "Every year we go through this ritual of developing a budget that we can include with the financial information packets to church members; but we're always guessing, because we do it before pledges are received."

"That also seems counterproductive since you place so much emphasis on tithing or proportionate giving," Mary said. "Doesn't giving people a copy of the proposed budget cause them to focus on where the money is going rather than on the concept of why the money is being given?"

"You're right. That's exactly what it does, and I really need to get the practice stopped. We ought to make out the budget after the pledges have been received. We have a couple of people on the finance commission who think members won't pledge if they don't have some idea where the money is going."

"But as you just said, 'most people don't give money to the line items of a budget.' I read material from one fund-raising consultant who said that most church members are really giving their money to people – to the people who are served by programs and to the people they trust to run the programs. Linking their giving to people is a way to deepen commitment for those who aren't able to see their giving as going directly to God."

"And let's face it," Brad observed, "giving to the church isn't the same as giving directly to God. We can't give the money directly to God. We have to give it through the church or through other nonprofit organizations, or we give it directly to people we know who are in need. Establishing those links is helpful. That's why we want people serving on the finance commission and conducting the annual campaign who are well respected, and the information we give members should make clear the kinds of people who benefit from the ministries of the church. It's especially good when we can give our members first-hand exposure to the needs which are met. Trips to mission sites, for example, are a very effective way to deepen their understanding of human need and their willingness to give generously."

"There's another level that affects the motivation of people for giving," Mary said. "Part of helping people with the spiritual motivation for giving is making them feel a part of the vision or mission of the church. When people are excited about where the church is going and what the church is doing, they're a lot more likely to dig deeply. Clear communication about the vision and mission of the church can help motivate people who are at a lot of different levels in their maturity on giving. It helps those who are spiritually mature, who think of giving as a response to God's generosity, and it also helps those who give primarily because they want to make a difference."

"Most of us are a mixture of motivations on giving. Those of us who are coming to think primarily of giving as a response to God's love still want to feel that our gifts are going to be well used and to get excited about the vision of the church. The more people who capture the vision of the church, the better. Simply sharing the budget of the church doesn't produce the same kind of excitement as a sense of vision."

Mission and Vision

In fact preparing a detailed budget in advance of a financial campaign can be counterproductive, since people will sometimes be critical of certain aspects of the budget. People give to bold visions of what the church will become, to broadly held understandings of the mission of the church, and to people about whom they care. The same people who may look at a line item for Sunday school materials and feel it represents too much money will look at a picture of a child being served by the church and respond generously.

While most of us can't avoid the use of terms like financial campaign, giving campaign, or fund-raising program, the reality is that what we are about is giving development rather than fund development. This affects the attitude with which we do everything. We want to develop people, not the budget. No matter what kind of campaign is being conducted, there will inevitably be follow-up to be done on those who did not respond with pledges or intentions of giving. When we approach those persons, we need to do so with the positive expectation of making new friends – not of collecting from deadbeats! The mental attitude with which we approach persons has everything to do with the result that we get.

Those who make major contributions to the church and to other charitable causes do not give so much to critical needs as to opportunities which are bold and dramatic. They will not be as moved by the fact that you are in danger of not making your routine budget as by the opportunity to be part of a new outreach to the community in which you minister. Not every financial crisis is a negative – at least that was the opinion of the congregational leaders we surveyed:

It seems to me that a financial crisis is not necessarily a negative if it results from the church taking its mission seriously and pushing ahead to meet needs. **80.5%** agreed

---

In general, congregations which are growing stretch their resources – seeking to make new ministries possible. They don't fall into the trap of continually having a financial crisis for which a special offering must be taken, since that can cause a lack of confidence from the membership; but they will risk having to come back for a special appeal rather than playing it so safe that they don't move forward with vision and mission. When the church has great enthusiasm, people will work hard and give generously to fulfill dreams and visions. The price of those dreams and visions may be an occasional financial crisis, but such churches can handle that. Simply avoid making the financial crisis a regular event!

Who Asks for Gifts?

Who asks for a gift can also make a difference. Churches which do every member visitations on a neighborhood basis rarely have the same level of success as churches which match carefully those who make the interpretive calls. People are much more positively motivated when approached by persons they know and when approached by persons who are at a slightly higher level of stewardship. That kind of matching also makes the visitation process more enjoyable for those persons making the calls.

If your church is using a cottage meeting approach or a carrier approach (pledge cards passed household to household as in the Pass-It-On approach), the question of *who* is still important. The composition of cottage meeting groups and of carrier groups does have impact on the final results. When you organize by neighborhood alone, you miss the benefits of grouping persons who can better motivate one another to higher levels of giving.

10. Help people give through their wills, living trusts, life insurance policies, and similar means.

This relates closely to number five which talks about providing opportunity for people to give from both checking and savings (from both current income and accumulated assets). This is sometimes referred to as "planned giving" and has become increasingly important for congregations and other religious organizations.

"If my church had done a better job in the past helping people remember it in their wills and living trusts," Jim said to Teresa, "we'd be better off today. Some of our members who have died just never considered the possibility of giving ten percent of their estates to the church. They give generously while alive but don't always think of it in planning for the distribution of their assets after their death."

"And sometimes the best distribution can be one that starts while they're still alive," Teresa said. "Our church-related colleges do a good job helping people be aware of the way charitable remainder trusts can help, but it never occurs to us to do that at the level of the congregation."

"We've started a new effort this year that we think will make a difference," Jim offered. "First, we're distributing a brochure about remembering the church in a person's will or living trust on the Sunday of Memorial Day weekend. Second, we're offering an estate

planning seminar in the fall for everyone but with a special appeal to persons who are fifty years of age and older. We have a top tax attorney sharing information with people. Third, we're writing to everyone in the last quarter of the year to remind them of various ways to help the church and to lower their own tax consequences. If we keep doing these things year-after-year, it will make a difference."

"That all sounds good," Teresa affirmed. "What we need to do in our congregation is relate those kinds of efforts to the establishment of an endowment fund. That would help people feel safer leaving large amounts of money to the church."

No One Lives Forever

No one lives forever. The clock keeps ticking for all of us. Our stewardship of the assets entrusted to us by God should include concern about what happens when we die. Sometimes assets can best be given while we are still alive; and in any event, the provision of a will, living trust, or other giving mechanism after death must be arranged during life.

The reality is that older members of most congregations today have more assets than younger members and also have more deeply held commitments to financial support of the church. The future giving plans of older members can help bridge the gap until younger members have acquired stronger habits of giving. In the Christian Community study, only 28% of the congregations had systematic programs to encourage people to remember the church financially in wills, living trusts, or similar legal instruments.

The probability of having a will or estate plan in effect increases as the age of the donor rises, running from 25% to 30% for those under thirty to 80% to 87% for those sixty-five or older. People are increasingly replacing wills with living trusts because of the probate avoidance which is often possible when a living trust has been properly constructed and implemented.

In encouraging people to include the church in their will or living trust, we should be sure to accomplish a couple of things:

1. We should suggest that people make at least a tithe of their estate. If that is the standard while living, then there is a certain consistency in considering that as a standard for one's estate. We also want to encourage persons to consider larger percentages than that, especially since there are some who do not have close family.

2. While designated giving is a helpful strategy on support of current needs of the congregation and can be a good way to handle memorial funds, people should be encouraged not to be overly specific in the use of funds given through a will or a living trust. Changes in the church and in the ministry situation could make it impossible to implement the specific desires of people. One certainly hopes for a significant time lapse between the time a will or living trust is prepared and the time that it is implemented! But things change with the passage of time. Thus, encourage those giving money through those instruments to avoid being too specific in designating what should be done. People should also be asked to include what is often called a "gift-over provision," which gives the church the authority to use the bequest or living trust proceeds in a prudent way if the donor's specified intent cannot be met.

Pastors can do much to encourage planned giving through wills, living trusts, appreciated assets, and other means. That includes making references to estate planning in sermons and giving people counsel on wills and estate planning. It's also important to celebrate what people have done. Several strategies in addition to wills and living trusts can be helpful.

An Assortment of Strategies

Life Insurance Policies make good gifts to charitable organizations. The money can be paid out to the charity far more quickly when the individual dies than can funds which must go through the probate process.

These are sometimes set up so that the church owns the life insurance policy and is the beneficiary, and they are sometimes established so that the donor retains ownership of the policy with the church as the beneficiary.

If your church is setting up an endowment fund and wants to give it a good jump-start, suggest that those involved in the planning process all take out life insurance policies with the endowment fund as the beneficiary. Especially if several people involved are relatively young, what people spend to begin the life insurance policies will be relatively small compared to the eventual benefit to the endowment fund. If ten persons each take out a $50,000 policy, you can announce $500,000 in gifts as the start of the endowment fund. This is a strategy recommended by some excellent professional fund-raisers.

A **Charitable Remainder Trust** is a gift to a charity which permits the giver to use the property and the income during his or her lifetime. At death, the property goes to the charity. The donor can receive a current deduction based on the value of the gift that the church will receive in the future – though IRS-set rates must be applied to discount that amount somewhat. This provides an immediate deduction, a continuing stream of income from what is in the trust, and the knowledge of substantial funds for the church in the future. **Charitable Lead Trusts** are a little different – the charity uses the property for a specified period of time and then it reverts back to the donor. The donor receives a one-time, up-front deduction for the income that will go to the church.

New tax laws, as of the date of this printing, have imposed some limitations on Charitable Remainder Trusts and Charitable Lead Trusts. They can still be good giving strategies, but be sure to consult an experienced accountant or attorney.

A **Revocable-Gift Agreement** lets the donor retain control and permits taking the funds back if needed. At the death of the donor, the funds become a permanent gift. No tax deduction is normally permitted at the time the agreement is made because of the donor retaining control.

The influence of your pastor and of other respected church leaders can do a lot to help people consider these options. When it comes to the specifics of arranging such gifts, the help of a good accountant or attorney is crucial.

More Strategies

One good way to promote memorial giving and will or living trust giving is to have a form which members are encouraged to complete. This form asks for information on how they want their memorial service handled including: the hymns they would like, the location, favorite Scripture passages, and the kinds of memorial gifts which would be most appealing. That form can be kept in the church files and is of significant help to the family and the church when a death occurs. At the same time that form is shared, people can receive information about remembering the church through a will or a living trust.

Another approach to planned giving comes in identifying persons felt to be capable of making significant gifts from assets and then sending one or two persons to visit with those prospective donors. For those not comfortable with such a direct approach, consider an informational program in Sunday school classes and small groups which includes a short survey for people to return if they are interested in visiting with someone about planned giving.

Federal and state regulations affecting wills, living trusts, charitable remainder trusts, life insurance gifts, and other strategies are always subject to change. You want the counsel of a competent attorney and/or accountant in any specific recommendations which you share with members of the church.

Memorial Service Planning Guide

We do not live to ourselves, and we do not die to ourselves. If we live, we live to the Lord, and if we die, we die to the Lord; so then, whether we live or whether we die, we are the Lord's. For to this end Christ died and lived again, so that he might be Lord of both the dead and the living. **Romans 14:7-9**

Name: _____

Address: _____

Phone: _____

Today's Date: _____

What is your preferred location for your memorial service (church, funeral home, or other)? _____

What requests do you have concerning music? This could include hymns you would like sung, special music, etc. _____

What requests do you have concerning Scripture, poetry, or other readings to be shared? Are there favorite passages of Scripture? Favorite poems?

Do you want the casket or ashes present for the memorial service? What other requests do you have concerning the handling of the body relative to the service?

What persons, if any, would you like to designate to share in your service (by reading Scripture, sharing words of reflection on your life, etc.)?

What other requests do you have concerning the memorial service?

What organizations would you like to receive gifts in your memory? Are there any kinds of projects you would especially like supported in your memory?

Most of us who have supported the church during our lives are also concerned about remembering the church in our wills or in our living trusts. If you would like to be contacted by someone from the church with more information on this, please check here: _____

Resources

Barna, George, **The Heart of the Donor** (Barna Research Group, 1995). Barna has always done good research, and this report of more than a thousand donors gives helpful insight into why people give and into how they feel about that giving. He makes some distinctions between the ways in which conservatives and liberals view their giving and the organizations they help.

Barna, George, **Raising Money for Your Church** (Barna Research Group, 1994). This guide to local church fund-raising draws on Barna's research about donors. You'll find a helpful blending of research with practical suggestions for improving giving in your congregation.

Barrett, Wayne C., **More Money, New Money, Big Money** (Discipleship Resources, 1992). Barrett is a respected professional who has done over a thousand on-site consultations with congregations. He gives especially helpful advice concerning the role of the pastor in stewardship education and in increasing giving. He correctly points out that the pastor is crucial to solving most of the problems that are barriers to effective stewardship, whether those are spiritual, leadership, or administrative. The book is filled with practical advice.

Berger, Hilbert J., **Now, Concerning the Offering** (Discipleship Resources, 1987, 1994). This very helpful book talks about the history and purpose of the offering and offers pragmatic strategies for improving this important part of the worship service.

Callahan, Kennon L., **Effective Church Finances** (HarperSanFrancisco, 1992). This is one of the most valuable books available on church finance and strongly emphasizes the relationship between giving campaigns and the mission of the church. He also does a great job explaining the different kinds of methods and strategies which can be employed in financial campaigns and the reasons for periodically changing those strategies.

Callahan, Kennon L., **Giving and Stewardship in an Effective Church** (HarperSanFrancisco, 1992). In this very practical book, Callahan shares basic principles of giving, sources of giving, and motivations for giving. He helps the reader understand why an annual campaign alone will not reach all the financial resources which are available.

Christian Century (407 S. Dearborn, Chicago, Illinois 60605-1150). This is an outstanding publication which includes thought-provoking articles on many aspects of ministry. You'll find more theological reflection here than in some of the other practice of ministry journals. The theological views of stewardship are especially helpful. John and Sylvia Ronsvalle (*Behind the Stained Glass Windows)* are among the contributors to this publication, and each issue includes an essay by Martin Marty.

Church Treasurer Alert (From Christian Ministry Resources, P.O. Box 1098, Matthews, North Carolina 28106). This newsletter comes out twelve times a year and has valuable information on accounting, financial, and tax developments of concern to churches and clergy. Issues contain information on such things as I.R.S. regulations on employees; suggested precautions in the handling of money; and suggestions on the kinds of reports needed by givers.

The Clergy Journal (6160 Carmen Avenue East, Inver Grove Heights, Minnesota 55076-4422). This ten-times a year publication is a journal specifically for clergy and covers a range of topics, including helpful articles on personal financial matters as well as church finances. There are several excellent contributors in the area of stewardship, including Thomas C. Rieke.

Congregations - The Alban Journal (From The Alban Institute, Suite 433 North, 4550 Montgomery Avenue, Bethesda, Maryland 20814-3341). This journal deals with the whole of congregational life, and there are frequent articles on stewardship which are always thought-provoking. Robert Wood Lynn and Dean R. Hoge have both shared recent articles with insights on giving in the local church. The Alban Institute, long under the leadership of Loren Mead and headed now by James P. Wind, provides excellent guidance on congregational life.

Hoge, Dean R., **Money Matters: Personal Giving in American Churches** (Westminster/John Knox, 1996). Dean Hoge is Professor of Sociology at Catholic University of America. Charles Zech, Patrick McNamara, and Michael J. Donahue are coauthors of this very helpful look at giving in our churches. You'll find perspective on differences in Protestant and Roman Catholic situations, and you'll also find considerable material for theological reflection on giving.

Ivie, Juanita L. and Donald W. Joiner, **Celebrate and Visit** (Discipleship Resources, 1990). This is a concise but very well-done guide to an every member visitation. You'll learn how to conduct an advance gifts campaign, how to recruit visitors, how to make effective use of minute speakers and testimonials, and more.

Joiner, Donald W., **Christians and Money** (Discipleship Resources, 1991). This is a well-prepared guide to personal finance which can be effectively used in stewardship education in your church. The book includes theological background, guidance in developing financial plans, suggestions for dealing with debt, and information on estate planning. This makes an excellent adult class study.

Joiner, Donald W. and Norma Wimberly, **The Abingdon Guide to Funding Ministry (Volume 1)** (Abingdon, 1995). This is the first of three volumes on funding ministry. This first volume offers an overall perspective on giving; the second volume deals with strategies for teaching about giving; and the third deals with proclaiming the joy of giving. This impressive volume pulls together a wide range of articles, suggestions, and strategies for giving. You'll find helpful material on the pastor's role in giving, on the importance of changing approaches to the annual campaign, on the establishment of endowment funds, and on government regulations pertaining to churches.

Journal of Stewardship (Published annually by the Ecumenical Center for Stewardship Studies, 1100 West 42nd Street, Suite 225, Indianapolis, Indiana 46208). This annual publication gets distributed through several denominations, so you may have some on your shelf. You'll find current statistics on church finances for several denominations and you'll also find an assortment of helpful resources for use in your stewardship program. These are always of high quality.

Leadership Journal (P.O. Box 37056, Boone, Iowa 50037-0056). Like the publications *Congregations, Net Results, Clergy Journal,* and *Your Church,* this journal deals with considerably more than stewardship. You'll find many helpful articles as well as reviews of resources. The Spring 1996 issue includes a very stimulating essay by Robert Russell about preaching on money. This publication often pulls together the best insights from evangelical and from mainline Protestants.

Levan, Christopher, **The Dancing Steward** (The United Church Publishing House, 1993). This is one of the most intellectually stimulating books available on stewardship. The author deals directly with the power that money plays in our lives and with our difficulty in breaking free of the possessive spirit which affects North American culture. Levan has a strong identity with the powerless in society and challenges us to change many of our preconceptions. Some of what the author says will sound radical to many, but this is a theologically solid book which deserves study.

Mather, Herb, **Don't Shoot the Horse ('Til You Know How to Drive the Tractor)** (Discipleship Resources, 1994). Herb Mather has been writing practical stewardship resources for many years, and this is one of his best. The thrust of the book is to move churches away from annual campaigns and over to a year-round emphasis on stewardship, but he doesn't recommend "shooting the horse" of the every member visitation too early in the transition. This would be a good book for study by a finance or stewardship commission.

Mather, Herbert and Donald W. Joiner, **Celebrate Together** (Discipleship Resources, 1989). This is a practical and helpful resource for conducting an annual campaign with the use of small groups. You'll find very specific guidance for the organization and promotion of the campaign.

Mather, Herbert and Donald W. Joiner, **Celebrate Giving** (Discipleship Resources, 1988, 1992). This gives guidance for an annual campaign centered around a Commitment Sunday. Worship services and telephone callers play key roles in this approach. You'll find the guidance you need for an effective campaign.

Mead, Loren B., **Transforming Congregations for the Future** (Alban Institute, 1994). This is a very frank book about the church by one of our most insightful religious thinkers. Mead correctly identifies and explains many of the problems and tensions in today's church. His chapter on "Roadblocks and Directions for the Journey" speaks clearly about the financial crisis in many churches and denominations.

Miller, Herb, **Consecration Sunday Stewardship Program** (Net Results/Abingdon, 1986, 1988, 1993, 1995). In our study, we found more congregations which had outstanding results using this program than any other packaged giving campaign resource. There are very clear step-by-step directions and also a very helpful accompanying cassette tape. For the program to work at its best, you need to follow all the steps which build to Consecration Sunday, including the use of an outside leader.

Net Results (Distributed by Cokesbury, 201 Eighth Avenue South, P.O. Box 801, Nashville, Tennessee 37202-0801). Herb Miller is the editor of this 12-times a year collection of ideas on church vitality and leadership. Each issue is packed with practical information from a wide range of sources, including articles from Lyle Schaller. You'll find much here to enhance all aspects of ministry, including stewardship.

Network for Charitable Giving (7700 Edgewater Drive, Suite 847, Oakland, California 9462). This is Thomas C. Rieke's organization. His name will be familiar to readers of many of the publications listed here, and he is one of the most experienced and knowledgeable people on church giving in the United States or Canada.

Resource Services, Inc., (12770 Merit Drive, Suite 900, Dallas, Texas 75251). This company offers three packaged annual campaigns which have generated good responses in the churches using them. Our survey found nothing but positive responses for churches using these resources: *The Joy of Belonging, Discover the Joy,* and *In the Light of Grace.*

Ronsvalle, John and Sylvia, **Behind the Stained Glass Windows: Money Dynamics in the Church** (Baker Books, 1996). This is perhaps the most thought-provoking book on stewardship to appear in recent years. John and Sylvia Ronsvalle conducted a study on church giving and developed a plan designed to create a uniform vision at the congregational level. The plan is a very demanding one, but it also produced some impressive results for those congregations which were able to successfully implement it. They raise important questions about the relationship between the rich and the poor and very articulately point out the difference that would be made by increased giving in our churches if those increases were directed to human need.

Roop, Eugene F., **Let the Rivers Run** (Wm. B. Eerdmans Publishing, 1991). This book is the one we most frequently recommend to congregations wanting to do class or group study to help members better understand the meaning of stewardship. Roop is the president of Bethany Theological Seminary and an outstanding biblical scholar. This book is easy to read, biblically based, and theologically sound. The author helps us develop a more mature understanding of the overall meaning of stewardship and teaches respect for the whole of creation. The book also contains great sermon material for pastors.

Schaller, Lyle E., **44 Ways to Expand the Financial Base of Your Congregation** (Abingdon, 1989, 1992). This is an excellent book filled with practical strategies and with sound reasons for those strategies. Those purchasing the book have permission to reproduce the great Friar Tuck cartoons by Edward Lee Tucker in local church publications.   You'll find guidance on special offerings, Miracle Sunday campaigns, capital fund-raising, planned giving, annual campaigns, and more. If you are only going to purchase one stewardship book in addition to the one you are holding in your hands, this should be the one.

Schaller, Lyle E., **Innovations in Ministry** (Abingdon, 1994). This is not a book about church finance as such but deals creatively with new models for ministry in the twenty-first century. He talks about new ways for congregations and denominations to deal with the paradigm shifts of our time and includes examples of churches making effective transitions to new patterns of ministry. This book has many financial implications for those working at the regional or national denominational levels and for pastors of churches looking for new approaches to ministry.

The Tithing Foundation   (79 W. Monroe, Suite 1021, Chicago, Illinois 60603-4907).   This organization provides a range of information on books, booklets, mailing and bulletin inserts, and video and audio cassettes – all of which promote tithing. The materials which they offer directly are available for remarkably low prices.

21st Century Strategies, Inc. (P.O. Box 549, Port Aransas, Texas 78373). This is Bill Easum's organization, and you can count on Bill to be on the cutting edge of local church renewal. Bill offers a stewardship program called "The Missing Piece" and a number of other helpful services.

Your Church (P.O. Box 8040, Wheaton, Illinois 60189). This publication comes free of charge to large numbers of clergy and churches and contains a large amount of advertising. Don't let that mislead you – this is a high quality publication which always has helpful material, often related to church finances. If you aren't on the list, you will want to be.

Complete Giving Campaign

Christian Community's *Complete Giving Campaign Program* draws on the extensive research reported in *The Desires of Your Heart* to provide your congregation with four carefully constructed options for conducting your annual giving commitment program. The entire program comes with permission to photocopy any part of it for use in your church. Because it provides four different campaigns, you can choose and adapt the most appropriate strategy for your congregation. Each one directly connects congregational giving to the development of the spiritual life. The four programs listed below help participants focus on the true desires of their hearts and recognize the centrality of commitment to Christ to all needs and desires.

The four strategies are:

Option 1: Cottage Meetings. Cottage meetings bring people together in relatively small groups to discuss congregational life, their own involvement in the church, and the place of giving in the development of the spiritual life. The meetings may be held in the homes of members, at the church, or in some combination of the two settings.

Option 2: Celebration Sunday. This approach uses a variety of strategies (including phone contacts and letters) to lead up to a Commitment Sunday which brings high attendance and high return of commitment cards.

Option 3: Pass It On. The Pass It On strategy centers on having bags of devotional materials, church information, and commitment cards pass from household to household throughout the congregation in a way that involves almost every resident member and constituent.

Option 4: Every Member Visitation. This approach involves trained volunteers who make visits to each household to interpret the church's needs, talk about the place of giving in the spiritual life, and urge improved levels of stewardship.

The *Complete Giving Campaign Program* provides:

- an explanation of the methodology of each strategy, covering its advantages and limitations, so that you may decide which strategy is most appropriate for your congregation.
- an outline covering every step and every necessary volunteer, all with careful explanations and defined roles.
- a responsibility sheet for each volunteer ready-made for photocopying.
- a checklist which helps you track your progress.
- letters to be sent out as dictated in the process outline, which can be immediately photocopied with **The Desires of Your Heart** letterhead or modified with your own congregation's letterhead.
- training materials for volunteers.
- stewardship education materials as appropriate for the program you choose which can be immediately photocopied with **The Desires of Your Heart** theme or modified with your own church's specific membership and financial information.
- *a computer disk with text files for many of the congregational materials.*

The *Complete Giving Campaign Program* is available for $89. As with any resource from Christian Community, you do not take any risk in ordering. You may return the complete program for a full refund if you are not delighted — and we're also glad to bill you if you would prefer to receive the resource before sending payment. An order form follows this page.

Response Form

Name: _____

Church: _____

Street/Box _____

City/State/Zip _____

Phone _____

Please check one:

___ My payment is enclosed, and Christian Community pays the postage and handling.

___ Please bill me. I agree to pay the actual shipping and handling, which is typically around 10-15% of the order total.

Please send me ___ **copies of** *The Desires of Your Heart* **report at $19 each.**

Please send me ___ **copies of** *The Desires of Your Heart Congregational Study Booklet,* a stewardship study guide designed for group or individual study based on *The Desires of Your Heart* report, at $7 each for 1–5 copies
$6 each for 6–10 copies
$5 each for 11 or more copies.

Please send me Christian Community's *Complete Giving Campaign Program* **at $89.** ___

Your satisfaction is guaranteed. Return the materials for a refund if you are not delighted.

If you would like more information about Christian Community's stewardship resources, please check as many areas as apply: ____ Receiving an On-Site Church Financial Check-up
____ Hosting a Church Finance Workshop
____ Attending a Church Finance Workshop
____ Receiving On-Site Financial Campaign Guidance

Return this form to:

Christian Community
6404 S. Calhoun Street
Fort Wayne, Indiana 46807
219-744-6510; e-mail DadofTia@aol.com